The Education Center®

From Your Friends at THE MAILBOX®

SING A SONG OF SEASONS

200 Original Songs, Poems, and Fingerplays

TABLE OF CONTENTS

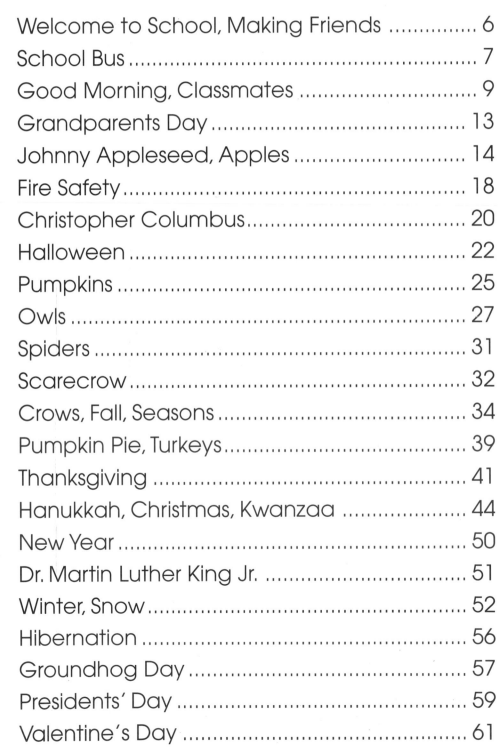

ABOUT THIS BOOK

Sing a Song of Seasons is a one-stop resource of over 200 child-centered songs, poems, and fingerplays. It fosters learning by combining the ease of familiar tunes or rhythms with the value of original lyrics that help you teach or reinforce your curriculum concepts. Lively, colorful illustrations relay the message of each song and provide samples of motions when needed. *Sing a Song of Seasons* is organized by season, making it easy for you to find just what you're looking for. So whether you're teaching about apples, Columbus Day, snow, or insects, reach for *Sing a Song of Seasons* to bring an abundance of lively learning into your early childhood classroom!

SING A SONG OF SEASONS

Managing Editor: Jan Trautman
Copy Editors: Sylvan Allen, Gina Farago, Karen Brewer Grossman, Karen L. Huffman, Amy Kirtley-Hill, Debbie Shoffner
Cover Artists: Nick Greenwood, Clevell Harris
Art Coordinator: Donna K. Teal
Artists: Pam Crane, Theresa Lewis Goode, Nick Greenwood, Sheila Krill, Clint Moore, Greg D. Rieves, Rebecca Saunders, Barry Slate, Stuart Smith, Donna K. Teal
Typesetters: Lynette Dickerson, Mark Rainey

President, The Mailbox Book Company™: Joseph C. Bucci
Director of Book Planning and Development: Chris Poindexter
Book Development Managers: Elizabeth H. Lindsay, Thad McLaurin, Susan Walker
Curriculum Director: Karen P. Shelton
Traffic Manager: Lisa K. Pitts
Librarian: Dorothy C. McKinney
Editorial and Freelance Management: Karen A. Brudnak
Editorial Training: Irving P. Crump
Editorial Assistants: Terrie Head, Hope Rodgers, Jan E. Witcher

www.themailbox.com

©2002 by THE EDUCATION CENTER, INC.
All rights reserved.
ISBN10 #1-56234-498-6 • ISBN13 #978-156234-498-6

Manufactured in the United States
10 9 8 7 6 5 4

FALL

WELCOME, WELCOME

Sing this song at the beginning of any school day, or rehearse it especially for times when a new student joins your class. Welcome!

(sung to the tune of "Old MacDonald Had a Farm")

Welcome, welcome to our class.
We're so glad you're here!
Welcome, welcome to our class.
We're so glad you're here!
Come on in and join the fun.
School is fun for everyone.
Welcome, welcome to our class.
We're so glad you're here!

—adapted from an idea by Deborah Garmon

EVERYBODY SHAKE HANDS

Mix and mingle to a tune that encourages new friendships!

(sung to the tune of "Old MacDonald Had a Farm")

Everybody, find a friend.
Get ready—one, two, three.
Everybody, find a friend.
It's easy—one, two, three.
Right hands out. All friends shake hands.
Everybody shaking, shaking hands.
Now find a new friend, look around.
Get ready—one, two, three!

Repeat from "Right hands out" as many times as you'd like. Then wrap up the song as follows:

Right hands out. All friends shake hands.
Everybody shaking, shaking hands.
Now everybody has a friend.
It's easy—one, two, three!

 FALL

WHEN THE BUS BRINGS US TO SCHOOL

Team a positive outlook on school with a review of transportation. Sing all about it!

(sung to the tune of "When the Saints Go Marching In")

Oh, when the bus brings us to school,
Oh, when the bus brings us to school.
Oh, we'll make a lot of new friends
When the bus brings us to school.

Oh, when the cars bring us to school,
Oh, when the cars bring us to school.
Oh, we'll make a lot of new friends
When the cars bring us to school.

Oh, when our feet walk us to school,
Oh, when our feet walk us to school.
Oh, we'll make a lot of new friends
When our feet walk us to school.

—Angie Kutzer

SCHOOL BUS RULES

A simple little melody packed with important information!

(sung to the tune of "Row, Row, Row Your Boat")

Ride, ride, ride the bus
Safely (to/from) our school.
Quiet voices, hands, and feet—
We obey the rules.

THE SCHOOL BUS SONG

Seat your students in chairs that have been arranged school bus–style. Then sing this song together, encouraging children to act it out.

(sung to the tune of "London Bridge")

Sing with me the school bus song,
School bus song, school bus song.
Sing with me the school bus song
And be a safe bus rider.

Always sit down in your seat,
In your seat, in your seat.
Always sit down in your seat
And be a safe bus rider.

Always use your quiet voice,
Quiet voice, quiet voice.
Always use your quiet voice
And be a safe bus rider.

Keep your two hands in your lap,
In your lap, in your lap.
Keep your two hands in your lap
And be a safe bus rider.

Listen when the driver speaks,
Driver speaks, driver speaks.
Listen when the driver speaks
And be a safe bus rider.

Walk when getting on and off,
On and off, on and off.
Walk when getting on and off
And be a safe bus rider.

—Cele McCloskey

GOOD MORNING!

(sung to the tune of "Good Night, Ladies")

Teacher sings:
Good morning, children.
Good morning, children.
Good morning, children.
I'm glad that you're all here!

Children sing:
Good morning, teacher.
Good morning, teacher.
Good morning, teacher.
We're glad we're here today!

Substitute your students' names for the names shown below and repeat the tune as necessary.

Everybody sings, with teacher pointing to children one by one:
David, Kendra, Shandra, Lateesha,Carter, and Cameron—
We're glad that you're all here!

DO YOU KNOW?

(sung to the tune of "The Muffin Man")

Do you know (Ms. Browning's) class,
(Ms. Browning's) class, (Ms. Browning's) class?
Do you know (Ms. Browning's) class?
Let's say the names together.

Matthew, Sharon, John, and Luke,
Seth, Michael, Becca, and Katie,
Cory, Brandon, Shayna, and Riley
Are in (Ms. Browning's) class.

Colleen, Phillip, James, and Shawna,
Carley, Tamika, Jerome, and Deidra,
Casey, Kristen, and Elizabeth
Are in (Ms. Browning's) class.

Yes, we know (Ms. Browning's) class,
(Ms. Browning's) class, (Ms. Browning's) class.
Yes, we know (Ms. Browning's) class.
We said the names together!

Substitute the names of your students and repeat the tune as necessary.

FRIENDS

(sung to the tune of "The More We Get Together")

Oh, friends who (<u>play</u>) together,
   together, together,
Oh, friends who (<u>play</u>) together will stay
   friends for sure!

Substitute a different action word each time you sing the song. Examples:

sing
share
work
learn

SPECIAL FRIEND

(Adapt this song to the tune of "Mary Had a Little Lamb")

Once I had a special friend, special friend,
Special friend.
Once I had a special friend who
(<u>Had a pink bow in her hair</u>).

Encourage children to guess the person you're singing about. Substitute a new clue for a different student each time you repeat the song. Examples:

Wore blue sneakers on his feet
Had a yellow T-shirt on
Wore a braid in her blonde hair
Liked to build with blocks

A VERY SPECIAL FRIEND

This song is perfect for the beginning of the year or the arrival of a new child in your class.

(sung to the tune of "The Muffin Man")

(Kelly) is a friend of ours,
A friend of ours, a friend of ours.
(Kelly) is a friend of ours—
A very special friend!

Repeat the song with a different student's name each time.

—Suzanne Moore

OUR GOOD FRIENDS

(sung to the tune of "Short'nin' Bread")

We have a good friend, good friend, good friend.
We have a good friend in our class.
(His) name is (Nathan, Nathan, Nathan).
(His) name is (Nathan), and he's in our class.

Repeat the song with a different student's name each time.

YOU ARE WELCOME

A little song goes a long way to help a newcomer feel welcome!

(sung to the tune of "Are You Sleeping?")

You are welcome, you are welcome
In our school, in our school.
We are glad to meet you—
Very glad to meet you.
Yes, we are! Yes, we are!

Where are you from? Where are you from?
Near or far? Near or far?
We are now your new friends.
We are now your new friends.
Yes, we are! Yes, we are!

—Colleen Dabney

OUR BRAND NEW FRIEND

A new child will be thrilled to hear her name in this affirming song.

(sung to the tune of "The Muffin Man")

Oh, do you know our brand-new friend,
Our brand-new friend, our brand-new friend?
Oh, do you know our brand-new friend
Who came to school today?

Yes, we know our brand-new friend,
Our brand-new friend, our brand-new friend.
Yes, we know our brand-new friend.
(Her) name is (Heather Carson).

—Ada Goren

GRANDPARENTS DAY

Hearts will be full when your students sing this song to grandparents or special older friends.

(sung to the tune of "Did You Ever See a Lassie?")

Oh, we want to show we love you,
We love you, we love you.
Oh, we want to show we love you
On Grandparents Day.

From this hand to
that hand,

From that hand to
this hand,

Oh, we want to show
we love you,
And this is how much!

—Roxanne LaBell Dearman

I LOVE MY GRANDPARENTS

Whether the grandparents come to the song or the song travels to them, they'll love this little number!

(sung to the tune of "Where Is Thumbkin?")

I love Grandma.
I love Grandma.
Yes, I do!
She loves me too!
I'll give her hugs and kisses
And many happy wishes
On Grandparents Day, Grandparents Day.

I love Grandpa.
I love Grandpa.
Yes, I do!
He loves me too!
I'll give him hugs and kisses
And many happy wishes
On Grandparents Day, Grandparents Day.

—Cynthia Holcomb

THANK YOU, JOHNNY!

(sung to the tune of "Clementine")

Thank you, Johnny.
Thank you, Johnny.
Thank you, Johnny Appleseed,
For the apple seeds you planted
That grew into apple trees.

Thanks for red ones.
Thanks for green ones.
Thanks for yellow apples too!
Thank you, Johnny, for the apples,
For the apples that you grew.

—Lucia Kemp Henry

JOHNNY APPLESEED

(sung to the tune of "Are You Sleeping?")

Johnny Appleseed,
Johnny Appleseed
Planted seeds,
Planted seeds.
Apple trees are growing,
Apple trees are growing
Everywhere!
Everywhere!

—Christy McClellan

THE JOHNNY APPLESEED SONG

(sung to the tune of "London Bridge")

Here comes Johnny Appleseed,
Appleseed, Appleseed.
Here comes Johnny Appleseed.
Here comes Johnny!

Plant the small seeds in the ground,
In the ground, in the ground.
Plant the small seeds in the ground.
Someday we'll have apples!

Soon the seeds will start to sprout,
Start to sprout, start to sprout.
Soon the seeds will start to sprout.
Someday we'll have apples!

Then the tree grows big and tall,
Big and tall, big and tall.
Then the tree grows big and tall.
Someday we'll have apples.

Pick an apple from the tree,
From the tree, from the tree.
One for you and one for me.
Thank you, Johnny!

—Cynthia Holcomb

APPLE COLORS

Here's a colorful little tune about apples!

(sung to the tune of "Three Blind Mice")

Red, yellow, green.
Red, yellow, green.
Growing on trees.
Growing on trees.
Sweet and crunchy and good for you.
They grow on trees in three colors, it's true!
Do you like apples? 'Cause I really do!
In red, yellow, and green.

—Ada Goren

APPLE OPTIONS

Oh, the abundance of apple appeal!
Sing the song below with your class,
substituting a different apple treat in the
last line each time. Later, encourage your
students to add their own suggestions!

(sung to the tune of "Bingo")

Apples falling from the trees—
What will we do now?
A-P-P-L-E, A-P-P-L-E, A-P-P-L-E,
We'll make (an apple pie)!

some applesauce
some apple crisp
some apple cider
some apple butter
some apple pancakes

—Cele McCloskey

THE APPLE CRUNCH

(sung to the tune of "The Hokey-Pokey")

I climb up in the tree.
I take a look around.
I spot one hanging there.
A shiny apple I have found.
I pick that juicy apple,
And I climb back to the ground.
Can't wait to hear that sound—CRUNCH!

Could be a Macintosh,
A Granny Smith, or Rome.
I like them all, you see.
I'll take any apple home.
I pick a juicy apple,
And I climb back to the ground.
Can't wait to hear that sound—CRUNCH!

—Angie Kutzer

FIRE SAFETY SONG

(sung to the tune of "Are You Sleeping?")

If your clothes should
Catch on fire,
Do not run!
Do not run!
Lie down on the ground and
Cover up your eyes. Then
Roll, roll, roll!
Roll, roll, roll!

—Heather Miller

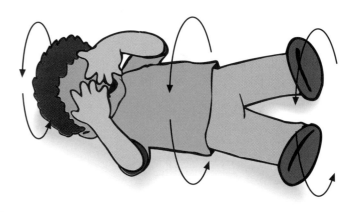

CALL FOR HELP!

(sung to the tune of "The Wheels on the Bus")

If there is a fire, stay low and go,
low and go, low and go!
If there is a fire, stay low and go.
Then call for help!

If there is a fire, get out, stay out;
Get out, stay out; get out, stay out!
If there is a fire, get out, stay out.
Then call for help!

If fire gets on you, just stop, drop, and roll;
Stop, drop, and roll; stop, drop, and roll.
If fire gets on you, just stop, drop, and roll.
Then call for help!

If there is a fire, call 9–1–1,
9–1–1, 9–1–1.
If there is a fire, call 9–1–1
And ask for help!

—Suzanne Moore

THE FIREFIGHTER

(sung to the tune of "If You're Happy and You Know It")

Oh, the firefighter drives a truck that's red,
And he wears a special helmet on his head.
When you dial 9-1-1,
He will grab his coat and run.
Oh, the firefighter drives a truck that's red.

Oh, the firefighter has a mighty hose,
And she wears her special fire-fighting clothes.
When you dial 9-1-1,
She will grab her coat and run.
Oh, the firefighter has a mighty hose.

Oh, the firefighter has a ladder tall.
He can climb up on the highest, highest wall.
When you dial 9-1-1,
He will grab his coat and run.
Oh, the firefighter has a ladder tall.

—Betty Silkunas

CHRISTOPHER COLUMBUS

(sung to the tune of "Did You Ever See a Lassie?")

Oh, Christopher Columbus, Columbus, Columbus,
Oh, Christopher Columbus
Had mighty ships three:
The Niña, the Pinta, the Santa María.
Oh, Christopher Columbus
Had mighty ships three.

Oh, Christopher Columbus, Columbus, Columbus,
Oh, Christopher Columbus
Found new land for us
With mountains and valleys and rivers and
    oceans.
Oh, Christopher Columbus
Found new land for us.

—Eva Bareis

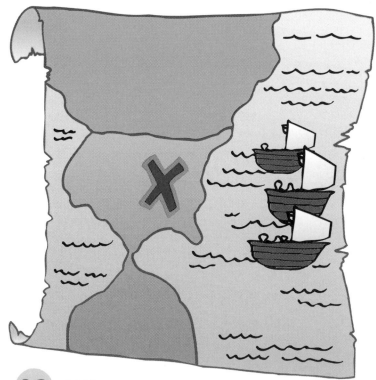

COLUMBUS DAY

(sung to the tune of "Five Little Ducks")

Columbus sailed the ocean blue
Back in 1492.
He had three ships,
And he sailed away.
This we remember on Columbus Day!
Columbus Day!
This we remember on Columbus Day!

—Ada Goren

IT'S CHRISTOPHER COLUMBUS!

(sung to the tune of "The Muffin Man")

Do you know who sailed the sea,
Across the sea
With sailboats three?
He found new land for you and me.
It's Christopher Columbus!

—Betty Silkunas

THREE SHIPS

(sung to the tune of "Yankee Doodle")

Columbus had three sailing ships.
He sailed across the ocean.
He sailed all day and sailed all night
Until he found America.

Niña, Pinta, Santa María
Niña, Pinta, Santa María
Niña, Pinta, Santa María—
They sailed across the ocean!

—Clevell Harris

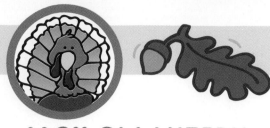

JACK-O'-LANTERN

*(sung to the tune of
"Twinkle, Twinkle, Little Star")*

First, we'll draw your eyes and nose.
Then a mouth with teeth in rows.
Cut you up and scoop you out.
Soon the neighborhood will shout—
As your light gives off its beam—
HAPPY, HAPPY HALLOWEEN!

—Cele McCloskey

PUMPKINS

*(sung to the tune of
"Yankee Doodle")*

Pumpkins, pumpkins,
Pick one out.
Scoop out all the seeds.
Carve a nose, two eyes, and mouth.
Oh, happy Halloween!

—Leigh Anne Rhodes

ONE, TWO
(poem)

One, two,
The kids say, "Boo!"
Three, four,
Knock on the door.
Five, six,
Bag of tricks.
Seven, eight,
Getting late.
Nine, ten,
A dressed-up friend.
Halloween is here again!

—Colleen Dabney

I'LL BE TRICK-OR-TREATIN'

(sung to the tune of "She'll Be Comin' Round the Mountain")

I'll be trick-or-treatin' soon on Halloween.
I'll be trick-or-treatin' soon on Halloween.
I'll be trickin', I'll be treatin',
And those treats I will be eatin'.
I'll be trick-or-treatin' soon on Halloween!

—Suzanne Moore

TRICK OR TREAT

(sung to the tune of "Jingle Bells")

Verse:
I wonder who I'll see
When I go out tonight,
When I go trick-or-treat
In the pale moonlight.
I'll wonder if it's you.
You'll wonder if it's me.
Oh, what fun it is to see
Who's out on Halloween!

Chorus:
Trick or treat! Trick or treat!
Just who will it be?
Oh, what fun it is to see who's out on Halloween!
Trick or treat! Trick or treat!
Just who will it be?
Oh, what fun it is to see who's out on Halloween!

—adapted from an idea by Eva Bareis

HALLOWEEN

Use this happily haunting Halloween song to encourage children to practice keeping a steady beat. As you sing together, invite children to march, move their arms, or create original movements to go along with the beat of the song.

(sung to the tune of "The Ants Go Marching")

Halloween is coming soon. Hurrah! Hurrah!
Halloween is coming soon. Hurrah! Hurrah!
Trick-or-treating and party cheer—
There is no spookier time of year.
And we all go marching
Down through the town
To go trick-or-treating.

Pumpkins growing everywhere. Hurrah!
  Hurrah!
Pumpkins growing everywhere. Hurrah!
  Hurrah!
Lumping the seeds in a gooey pile,
Then carving two eyes and a great big
  smile.
And we all go marching
Down through the town
To go trick-or-treating.

Ghosts and goblins fly through the night.
  Hurrah! Hurrah!
Ghosts and goblins fly through the night.
  Hurrah! Hurrah!
Look to the sky. It's an awesome sight!
The sky is black and the moon is bright.
And we all go marching
Down through the town
To go trick-or-treating. Hey!

—Michelle McCormick

A HALLOWEEN MISTAKE

(poem)

I cannot move my arms or legs.
I cannot move my feet.
And really I need all of them
When I trick-or-treat.

I'm wrapped up in a tube sock
That's huge and painted green.
I guess it's not too smart to be
A snake for Halloween!

—Rusty Fischer

SING A SONG OF PUMPKINS

(sung to the tune of
"Sing a Song of Sixpence")

Sing a song of pumpkins
Nice and big and round,
Growing in the pumpkin patch
All around the ground.
I'll pick out my pumpkin
And scoop it nice and clean,
Then carve a jack-o'-lantern.
Oh, happy Halloween!

—Suzanne Moore

PUMPKINS EVERYWHERE!

If you have child-made pumpkins of all shapes and sizes displayed around your classroom, here's a perfect follow-up song. If your students haven't yet started their festive fall art endeavors, use the song for artistic inspiration!

(sung to the tune of
"Old MacDonald Had a Farm")

Pumpkins, pumpkins all around,
Pumpkins everywhere!
Pumpkins, pumpkins on the ground,
Lots of them to share!
Some are big.
Some are small.
Fat ones, skinny ones,
Some are even quite tall!
Pumpkins, pumpkins all around.
Pumpkins everywhere!

—Deborah Garmon

THE PUMPKIN SEED

(sung to the tune of "The Itsy-Bitsy Spider")

Once the little
pumpkin seeds
Were planted in
the ground.

Down came the
raindrops,
Falling all
around.

Out came the
sun
And vines began
to grow.

Then after yellow
flowers
The pumpkins
grew just so!

—Jana Sanderson

Surprised
jack-o'-lantern

WHERE'S MY PUMPKIN?

Use this seasonal song to help reinforce the concept of feelings. As children sing this song, invite them to dramatize the type of face that is indicated in the blank. Repeat the song as often as you'd like, substituting a different feeling word each time.

(sung to the tune of "Where Is Thumbkin?")

Where's my pumpkin? Where's my pumpkin?
Here it is! Here it is!
(Happy) jack-o'-lantern.
(Happy) jack-o'-lantern.
Looks like this. Looks like this.

—Margaret Southard

SLEEPING OWL

This simple little song does big things to help teach the idea that owls are nocturnal birds.

(sung to the tune of "Are You Sleeping?")

Are you sleeping,
Are you sleeping,
Mrs. Owl, Mrs. Owl?
You sleep during daylight;
Then you stay up all night.
"Whoo, whoo, whoo!"
"Whoo, whoo, whoo!"

—Deborah Garmon

THE OWL

(sung to the tune of "Row, Row, Row Your Boat")

Flap, flap, flap your wings
In the dark of night.
"Whoo, whoo, whoo, whoo!"
Flying through the night.

Rest, rest, rest your head
In the light of day.
"Whoo, whoo, whoo, whoo!"
Sleeping through the day.

—Christy McClellan

OWL'S NIGHT AND DAY

Once your little ones are familiar with this song, try this accompanying activity for some role-playing fun! Divide your class into two groups. Have half of the class sing the song while the other half acts it out. Then invite the groups to switch roles and sing and act out the song again. Now let me get this straight—they sleep during the *day*?

(sung to the tune of "Are You Sleeping?")

Are you sleeping,
Are you sleeping,
Little owl, little owl?
Wake up now it's nighttime.
Wake up now it's nighttime.
Fly away! Fly away!

Go to sleep now.
Go to sleep now,
Little owl, little owl.
Time to close your eyes now.
Time to close your eyes now.
Sleep away, through the day.

—Linda Masternak Justice

LOOK! THERE'S AN OWL
(poem)

Look! There's an owl sitting in the tree.

He has great big eyes and he's looking at me!

Look! There's an owl in the bright moon-light.

He sleeps through the day and stays up through the night.

Look! There's an owl. See his head turn around.

And if you listen very closely you can hear this sound—

Whooo! Whooo! Whooo!

—Heather Graley

I'M A LITTLE OWL

(sung to the tune of "I'm a Little Teapot")

I'm a little owl
Old and wise,
With one sharp beak
And two big eyes.
When the moon comes out
I sing my song:
"Hoot, hoot, hoot!"
Won't you sing along?

—Julie A. Koczur

BARN OWL BREAKFAST

If you're studying owls, this song helps review the barn owl's diet. Copy the song on chart paper. Then ask your students to brainstorm a list of things a barn owl might eat. As you sing the song, substitute a different word from the list each time. This is life science in a song!

(sung to the tune of "Row, Row, Row Your Boat")

Barn owl flies at night
Searching for his prey.
Watch out, (<u>field mouse</u>),
He spies you there.
You'd better run away!

—Roxanne LaBell Dearman

Today's Menu

gopher	frog
rat	lizard
rabbit	bird
bat	insects

LITTLE OWL

(sung to the tune of "Twinkle, Twinkle, Little Star")

Little owl awake all night,
We don't see you in broad daylight.
When the moon is high and bright,
Little owl takes to flight.
Little owl awake all night,
We don't see you in broad daylight.

—Cynthia Holcomb

THAT'S WHAT SPIDERS DO

*(sung to the tune of
"Row, Row, Row Your Boat")*

Spin, spin, spin a web,
That's what spiders do.
Round and round and up and down,
They spin their webs, it's true.

Catch, catch, catch a bug,
That's what spiders do.
In their sticky spiderwebs
They catch some bugs, it's true.

—Ada Goren

THE SPIDER SPINS A WEB

*(sung to the tune of
"The Farmer in the Dell")*

The spider spins a web.
The spider spins a web.
Up, down, and all around,
The spider spins a web.

The web traps a (fly).
The web traps a (fly).
Up, down, and all around,
The web traps a (fly).

The spider eats the (fly).
The spider eats the (fly).
Up, down, and all around,
The spider eats the (fly).

*Encourage children to repeat the song,
each time substituting a different insect
that the spider might trap in its web.*

—Christy McClellan

EIGHT LITTLE LEGS

(sung to the tune of "Ten Little Indians")

One little, two little, three little legs,
Four little, five little, six little legs,
Seven little, eight little legs on me.
That makes me an *arachnid!*

I'M A SCARY SCARECROW

(sung to the tune of "I'm a Little Teapot")

I'm a scary scarecrow, tall and straight.
I stand all day by the cornfield gate.
Those black and noisy crows, they don't scare me.
For I scare them with a ONE, TWO, THREE! BOO!

—Betty Silkunas

MUST BE SCARECROW

(sung to the tune of "Must Be Santa")

Who's got a checkered scarf of red?
Scarecrow's got a checkered scarf of red.
Who wears an old hat on his head?
Scarecrow wears an old hat on his head.
Hat on head, scarf of red—
Must be Scarecrow. Must be Scarecrow.
Must be Scarecrow, this we know!

Who's got a body stuffed with straw?
Scarecrow's got a body stuffed with straw.
Who hears the crows go "Caw! Caw! Caw!"
Scarecrow hears the crows go "Caw! Caw! Caw!"
"Caw! Caw! Caw!", stuffed with straw, hat on head,
    scarf of red—
Must be Scarecrow. Must be Scarecrow.
Must be Scarecrow, this we know!

Who's in the cornfield all the day?
Scarecrow's in the cornfield all the day.
Who scares the hungry crows away?
Scarecrow scares the hungry crows away.
Crows away, all the day, "Caw! Caw! Caw!",
    stuffed with straw, hat on head, scarf of red—
Must be Scarecrow. Must be Scarecrow.
Must be Scarecrow, this we know!

—Lucia Kemp Henry

WHERE IS BLACK CROW?

(sung to the tune of "Where Is Thumbkin?")

Where is black crow?
Where is black crow?
Here I am!
Here I am!
I landed on your (<u>elbow</u>).
I landed on your (<u>elbow</u>).
Off I go!
Off I go!

Repeat the song, substituting a different body part each time.

—Jana Sanderson

FALL IS COMING

(sung to the tune of "Are You Sleeping?")

Fall is coming. Fall is coming.
Look and see! Look and see!
The leaves are changing colors
And they've started falling
From the trees, from the trees.

—Leigh Anne Rhodes

FOUR SEASONS

(sung to the tune of "This Old Man")

Winter, spring,
Summer, fall,
There are four seasons in all.
They bring us snow and wind and rain and sun.
Every season has some fun!

—Ada Goren

FOUR IN ONE

(sung to the tune of "Clementine")

Four seasons, four seasons,
Four seasons in one year.
Spring then summer,
Fall then winter,
Four seasons in one year.

—Susan DeRiso

SEASONS CHANGE THE WORLD

(sung to the tune of "London Bridge")

Seasons come and seasons go,
Come and go, come and go.
Seasons come and seasons go.
Watch the world a-changing.

In the springtime rain does fall,
Rain does fall, rain does fall.
In the springtime rain does fall.
Watch the world a-changing.

Summer heat means we can swim,
We can swim, we can swim.
Summer heat means we can swim.
Watch the world a-changing.

Falling leaves are autumn's call,
Autumn's call, autumn's call.
Falling leaves are autumn's call.
Watch the world a-changing.

Snowy days mean winter's here,
Winter's here, winter's here.
Snowy days mean winter's here.
Watch the world a-changing.

Seasons come and seasons go,
Come and go, come and go.
Seasons come and seasons go.
Watch the world a-changing.

—Cele McCloskey

SEASONS SONG

(sung to the tune of "She'll Be Comin' Round the Mountain")

In wintertime the weather gets so cold. (Brr-rrr!)
In wintertime the weather gets so cold. (Brr-rrr!)
In wintertime it's freezin'
And the reason is the season.
Oh, in wintertime the weather gets so cold. (Brr-rrr!)

In the spring the weather warms and flowers bloom. (Oooh-ahhhh!)
In the spring the weather warms and flowers bloom. (Oooh-ahhhh!)
In spring the bloomin' flowers
Get watered by rain showers.
Oh, in spring the weather warms and flowers bloom.
(Oooh-ahhhh! Brr-rrr!)

In summertime the weather gets so hot. (Phew-wee!)
In summertime the weather gets so hot. (Phew-wee!)
In the summertime it's hot
And we're in the pool a lot.
Oh, in summertime the weather gets so hot.
(Phew-wee! Oooh-ahhhh! Brr-rrr!)

In fall the weather cools and leaves fall down. (Swish! Swish!)
In fall the weather cools and leaves fall down. (Swish! Swish!)
In fall the leaves are fallin'
And we rake 'em and we haul 'em.
Oh, in fall the weather cools and leaves fall down.
(Swish! Swish! Phew-wee! Oooh-ahhhh! Brr-rrr!)

I LIKE FALL

(sung to the tune of "This Old Man")

I like fall.
I like leaves.
I like apples on the trees.
Oh, that cool fall air can really make me smile.
I'm glad fall's here for a while!

—Ellen Butorac

FALL IS FINALLY HERE

The predictable and repetitive text in this song make it a great choice for group sings-alongs or independent read-the-room activities.

(sung to the tune of "The Farmer in the Dell")

Fall is finally here.
Fall is finally here.
Leaves fall down
And blow around.
Fall is finally here.

Fall is finally here.
Fall is finally here.
Leaves fall down
Yellow, orange, and brown.
Fall is finally here.

Fall is finally here.
Fall is finally here.
Leaves fall down
And cover the ground.
Fall is finally here.

—Peggy Campbell-Rush

THIS IS THE WAY THE LEAVES FALL DOWN

Here's a simple song with big vocabulary-building opportunities!

(sung to the tune of "Row, Row, Row Your Boat")

(Float, float, float) right down
Gently to the ground.
This is the way the leaves fall down
All around the town.

Whirl, whirl, whirl
Twirl, twirl, twirl
Swish, swish, swish
Blow, blow, blow
Drift, drift, drift

—Peggy Campbell-Rush

PUMPKIN PIE

(sung to the tune of "Short'nin' Bread")

Everybody likes to make pumpkin, pumpkin,
Everybody likes to make pumpkin pie!

Mix in the pumpkin. Mix in the spice.
Bake it in the oven and it smells so nice!

Everybody likes to eat pumpkin, pumpkin,
Everybody likes to eat pumpkin pie!

—Lucia Kemp Henry

TURKEY HUNT
(poem)

As you read or recite this poem together, encourage your students to make up motions to go along with the text. A happy ending here for one and all!

Once I had a turkey
With feathers big and wide,
And when I tried to catch him,
He ran away to hide!

And so I lost my turkey
With feathers big and wide,
But when I "gobble-gobbled,"
He came back to my side!

—Eva Bareis

FIVE TURKEY STRUT

Have each child hold up five fingers and then fold them down, one at a time, as the class reads or recites this fingerplay. For the last line, have each child open all his fingers and fly them away. Ready?

Five fat turkeys strutted on the barnyard floor.
One spied Mr. Farmer and ran right out the door!

Four fat turkeys strutted as proud as they could be.
One saw Mrs. Farmer and quickly he did flee!

Three fat turkeys strutted a strut that's new.
One heard knives a-sharpenin' and he knew what to do!

Two fat turkeys strutted in the autumn sun.
One heard leaves a-cracklin' and he began to run!

One fat turkey strutted with nothing left to do.
Thanksgiving was a-coming so away he flew!

—adapted from an idea by Betty Silkunas

I'M A LITTLE TURKEY

(sung to the tune of "I'm a Little Teapot")

I'm a little turkey, plump and wide,

Feet on the bottom,

Wings on the side.

When I walk, I wobble to and fro.

Hear me gobble as off I go!

—Susan DeRiso

JUST BEFORE THANKSGIVING DAY

(sung to the tune of "Five Little Ducks")

Just before Thanksgiving day,
(Five) little turkeys ran away.
But the one who walked with a wibble and a wobble,
He led the others with a "gobble, gobble, gobble,
Gobble, gobble, gobble!"

Repeat the song, counting down, substituting one number less each time.

Last verse:
Just before Thanksgiving day,
One little turkey ran away.
When he called to the others with a "gobble, gobble, gobble,"
They all came back with a wibble and wobble, a wibble and wobble!

—Lucia Kemp Henry

THANKSGIVING

(sung to the tune of "Take Me Out to the Ballgame")

It's almost time for Thanksgiving;
It's almost time for a feast!
Turkey, potatoes, and corn bread too!
I just love pumpkin pie—don't you too?
Oh, it's almost time for Thanksgiving;
Oh, I don't think I can wait!
So give thanks for all that you have
And let's celebrate!

—Ada Goren

ON THANKSGIVING DAY

(sung to the tune of "If You're Happy and You Know It")

Do you (<u>eat some turkey</u>) on Thanksgiving Day?
Do you (<u>eat some turkey</u>) on Thanksgiving Day?
Well, no matter what you do,
Just be thankful through and through.
Do you (<u>eat some turkey</u>) on Thanksgiving Day?

travel someplace
hug your family
play some football
say, "I love you!"
help your mom

—Lucia Kemp Henry

COME AND SPIN THE DREIDEL

(sung to the tune of "The More We Get Together")

Oh, come and spin the dreidel, the dreidel, the dreidel.
Oh, come and spin the dreidel and see what you get.
You might have to give some,
Or maybe you'll win some.
Oh, come and spin the dreidel and see what you get!

—Ada Goren

HANUKKAH IS HERE!

(sung to the tune of "Mary Had a Little Lamb")

Let's light the menorah, menorah, menorah.
Let's light the menorah, for Hanukkah is here!

One candle each joyous night, joyous night, joyous night.
One candle each joyous night, for Hanukkah is here!

Latkes, games, and family, family, family.
Latkes, games, and family, for Hanukkah is here!

Let's light the menorah, menorah, menorah.
Let's light the menorah, for Hanukkah is here!

CHRISTMAS WISHES

(sung to the tune of "The Hokey-Pokey")

When Christmastime is here,
It's time for hope and cheer.
It's time for peace and joy
Toward every girl and boy.
I wish the same for you and your whole family.
That's Christmas to you from me!

S-A-N-T-A!

(sung to the tune of "Bingo")

He's jolly with a long white beard,
And just what is his name-o?
S-A-N-T-A! S-A-N-T-A! S-A-N-T-A!
And Santa is his name-o!

He laughs like this with a "Ho! Ho! Ho!"
And just what is his name-o?
S-A-N-T-A! S-A-N-T-A! S-A-N-T-A!
And Santa is his name-o!

He has reindeer that number eight,
And just what is his name-o?
S-A-N-T-A! S-A-N-T-A! S-A-N-T-A!
And Santa is his name-o!

His helpers are those little elves,
And just what is his name-o?
S-A-N-T-A! S-A-N-T-A! S-A-N-T-A!
And Santa is his name-o!

REINDEER WANNA-BE

(sung to the tune of "Oscar Mayer Weiner Song")

Oh, I wish that I were one of Santa's reindeer,
Helping pull his sleigh all filled with toys.
'Cause, oh, if I were one of Santa's reindeer,
I'd bring joy to lots of girls and boys!

—Ada Goren

SANTA'S REINDEER

(sung to the tune of "Are You Sleeping?")

Santa's reindeer, Santa's reindeer,
Off they go! Off they go!
Flying over rooftops,
Making all the house stops.
Ho! Ho! Ho!
Ho! Ho! Ho!

—Susan DeRiso

DECORATE THE TREE

(sung to the tune of "Kookaburra")

Hang (<u>a candy cane</u>) on the Christmas tree.
Decorate each branch with your family.
String lights upon it.
Put tinsel on it.
Decorate the tree!

popcorn string
a shiny star
an ornament
a teddy bear
an angel bright

—Lucia Kemp Henry

SING A SONG OF CHRISTMAS

(sung to the tune of "Sing a Song of Sixpence")

Sing a song of Christmas,
A season full of cheer.
Santa will be coming with eight of his reindeer.
The windows will be lit by glowing candlelight.
And carolers will carol in the moonglow at night!

Sing a song of Christmas,
A season full of joy.
Surprises wrapped in packages
For every girl and boy.
The Christmas tree is twinkling in the dark of night.
Oh, how I wish that Christmas would happen every night!

JINGLE, JINGLE

Invite a few children at a time to gently shake jingle bells as your whole class sings this song together. The perfect accompaniment!

(sung to the tune of "Are You Sleeping?")

Jingle, jingle. Jingle, jingle.
Jingle bells! Jingle bells!
I hear bells a-ringing.
Jing-a-ling-a-ling-ing.
Jingle bells! Jingle bells!

CHRISTMAS MORNING

(sung to the tune of "This Old Man")

Candy canes, snowy lanes,
Frost is on the windowpane.
And I can't wait to look under the tree
To see what Santa brought for me!

Toys and noise, Christmas joys,
Fun for every girl and boy.
But most of all there's love and family
At Christmastime around the tree!

KWANZAA

(sung to the tune of "Ten Little Indians")

One little, two little, three little candles,
Four little, five little, six little candles,
Seven little candles shine for Kwanzaa,
Shining in the kinara.

Three little red and three little green ones.
Black in the middle shines a little taller.
Shine little candles, shine for Kwanzaa,
Shining in the kinara.

—Clevell Harris

HOLIDAY LIGHT

(sung to the tune of "Daisy, Daisy")

Candles glowing in the soft dark of night.
Candles glowing, spreading a gentle light.
The holidays are upon us.
The feelings are so joyous.
So spread the light
And joy tonight,
Little holiday friend of mine!

NEW YEAR

(sung to the tune of "Rise and Shine")

Stand up and cheer!
The new year is here, is here!
Stand up and cheer!
The new year is here, is here!
Stand up and cheer!
The new year is here, is here!
It's a brand-new year!

—Ada Goren

NEW YEAR COUNTDOWN

(sung to the tune of "Did You Ever See a Lassie?")

Let's celebrate the new year, the new year, the new year.
Let's celebrate the new year as it comes around.
Blow horns; throw confetti.
Wear hats; then get ready
To begin the new year countdown from ten down to one.

Children chant:
Ten, nine, eight, seven, six, five, four, three, two, one…HAPPY NEW YEAR!

—Lucia Kemp Henry

A SONG OF PEACE

(sung to the tune of "Sing a Song of Sixpence")

Sing a song of peace for friendship everywhere.
Sing a song of peace to show you really care.
Sing a song of peace and hold it in your heart.
Isn't that the perfect place for peace to have its start?

—Susan DeRiso

OH, DR. KING

(sung to the tune of "O Christmas Tree")

Oh, Dr. King, he had a dream,
A dream of peace and freedom.
Oh, Dr. King, he had a dream,
A dream of peace and freedom.
He dreamed America would be
A land filled with equality.
Oh, Dr. King, he had a dream,
A dream of peace and freedom.

—Lucia Kemp Henry

TWO WARM MITTENS

This song is a great one to help facilitate the bundling up process on a cold winter day. Lots of skills here for your very young ones!

(sung to the tune of "He's Got the Whole World in His Hands")

I have two warm mittens on my hands.
I have two warm mittens on my hands.
I have two warm mittens on my hands.
They keep me cozy on a winter day!

—Ada Goren

TICKLE FACE SNOWFLAKES
(poem)

Snowflakes falling through the air,
Slowly drifting everywhere,
On my nose and on my chin.
If I open my mouth,
They fall right in!

—Heather Miller

SNOW FUN

Teach your children the song below. Once they are familiar with it, encourage students to brainstorm other snow activities to sing about in the fourth line. The snow fun has just begun!

(sung to the tune of "We Wish You a Merry Christmas")

Oh, I wish that it were snowing.
Oh, I wish that it were snowing.
Oh, I wish that it were snowing;
Then I'd (ride my sled)!

build a fort
make an angel
shovel my driveway
build a snowman

—Ada Goren

SNOWMAN SURPRISE

(sung to the tune of "Row, Row, Row Your Boat")

Roll, roll, roll the snow
To just the perfect size.
A nose, a mouth, and two black eyes—
You made a snow surprise!

—Susan DeRiso

SEE THE SNOWFLAKES

(sung to the tune of "London Bridge")

See the snowflakes falling down,
(Falling) down, (falling) down.
See the snowflakes falling down.
(Falling) snowflakes.

Repeat the song, replacing the underlined word with a new word each time, such as drifting, swirling, floating, or blowing.

—Lucia Kemp Henry

SNOW DAY!

(sung to the tune of "Up on the Housetop")

First come the snowflakes falling
    down,
Floating softly to the ground.
Then come the children ready
    to play,
Sliding, sledding—out all day!
Snow! Snow! Snow! Who
    wouldn't go?
Snow! Snow! Snow! Who
    wouldn't go?
Out in the snowflakes, yes sirree!
Out in the snowflakes, you and
    me!

—Susan DeRiso

FIVE LITTLE SNOWMEN

(poem)

After introducing this poem, assign each of the five snowmen described in this poem to a different child (or small group of children). Give each child a wooden paint stirrer and then invite her to use construction paper and a variety of art supplies to create a snowman stick puppet depicting the characteristics of the snowman assigned to her. When you read/recite the poem together, have each child manipulate her snow puppet when it is mentioned in the poem.

Five little snowmen standing in one place.
The first one said, "I have a frosty face."
The second one said, "I have a nippy nose."
The third one said, "I have ten cold toes!"
The fourth one said, "It's *freezing* here, you know!"
And the fifth one said, "I think it's time to go!"
"Yes! Yes!" said the snowmen. "We're freezing standing still!"
So the five little snowmen rolled down the hill!

—Lucia Kemp Henry

HIBERNATION

(sung to the tune of "Clementine")

Hibernation, hibernation,
When animals fall fast asleep.
Snug and warm all through the winter
In their cozy dens asleep.

—Lucia Kemp Henry

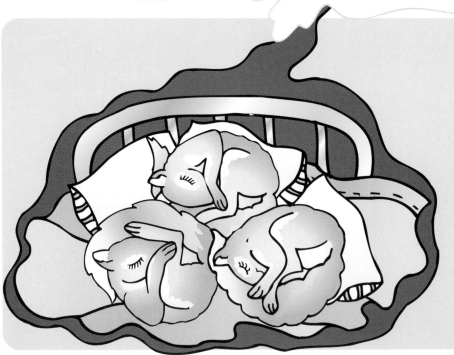

SLEEP, SLEEP, SLEEP

(sung to the tune of "Row, Row, Row Your Boat")

Sleep, sleep, sleep all day
And all through the night.
That's how animals hibernate.
They sleep both day and
    night.

—Ada Goren

I'M A LITTLE GROUNDHOG

Encourage your little ones to act out this song as you sing it together. Ready, everyone? We're groundhogs!

(sung to the tune of "I'm a Little Teapot")

I'm a little groundhog, furry and round.

I sleep so soundly in the ground.

On February 2, I will wake

With a yawn and a stretch and a shake, shake, shake!

I'll creep out of my hole and peek around

To look for my shadow on the ground.

If the coast is clear, I'm out to stay.

And sunny spring is on its way!

But if, when I am looking all around,

I spy my shadow on the ground,

I'll run right back into my winter hole

With six more weeks of winter to go!

—adapted from an idea by Susan DeRiso

GROUNDHOG DAY!

(sung to the tune of "Bingo")

When Mr. Groundhog takes a peek,
Oh, will he see his shadow?
Is spring on the way?
Or will winter stay?
Oh, I can hardly wait to see what Groundhog sees!

If Mr. Groundhog takes a peek,
And does not see his shadow,
Spring is on the way.
Winter goes away.
Oh, I can hardly wait to see what Groundhog sees!

If Mr. Groundhog takes a peek,
And there he sees his shadow,
Winter's here to stay.
Spring will be delayed.
Oh, I can hardly wait to see what Groundhog sees!

—Ada Goren

GROUNDHOG GRUFFLE

Sure, it might be a made-up word, but your youngsters will have no trouble acting out a groundhog's "gruffle." Try it and see!

(sung to the tune of "The Hokey-Pokey")

The little groundhog peeks
To see the coast all clear.
If spring is on the way, he'll give
    a groundhog cheer.
But if he sees his shadow he will
    "gruffle" and he'll grunt.
That groundhog is "outta" here!

THANK YOU, MR. PRESIDENT

(sung to the tune of "The Mulberry Bush")

Today we remember our presidents,
Presidents, presidents.
Today we remember our presidents.
Thank you, Mr. Washington!

Today we remember our presidents,
Presidents, presidents.
Today we remember our presidents.
Thank you, Mr. Lincoln!

Repeat the song as often as desired, substituting a different president's name in the last line each time.

—Susan DeRiso

PRESIDENTS' DAY

Give a melody to the facts and the learning is simple!

(sung to the tune of "My Country 'Tis of Thee")

Lincoln and Washington,
We will remember
On Presidents' Day.
Two men in history
Who gave us liberty.
Honor their memories
On this great day!

—Lori McGinnis

PRESIDENTIAL TRIBUTE

If you're performing this tribute for an audience, have groups of children hold up child-decorated cutouts corresponding to each verse of the song.

(sung to the tune of "The Wheels on the Bus")

Today we honor the presidents,
Presidents, presidents.
Today we honor the presidents
Who made our country great.

We remember George Washington,
Washington, Washington.
We remember George Washington,
The Father of Our Country.

We remember Abe Lincoln, too,
Lincoln, too, Lincoln, too.
We remember Abe Lincoln, too,
Who helped to free the slaves.

We honor both these presidents,
Presidents, presidents.
We honor both these presidents
On Presidents' Day!

—Ada Goren

PUNNY VALENTINE

Your kids will get the joke in this very punny valentine song! A good one to copy onto chart paper and use for read-the-room activities.

(sung to the tune of "The Farmer in the Dell")

Do you  all for me?
Do you carrot all for me?
I'd like to be your valentine.
Do you carrot all for me?

Does your heart beet for me?
Does your heart beet for me?
I'd like to be your valentine.
Does your heart beet for me?

We'd make a happy pear.
We'd make a happy pear.
I'd like to be your valentine.
We'd make a happy pear.

Lettuce just be friends.
Lettuce just be friends.
I'd like to be your valentine.
Lettuce just be friends.

VALENTINE WISHES

A kind thought goes a long way with this sweet song. To start the song going, insert a child's name when you get to the blank. Each time the song is repeated, the last child mentioned fills in the blank the next time around.

(sung to the tune of "Jingle Bells")

Valentine, valentine,
Won't you please be mine?
How I wish that (Allison)
Would be my valentine! Oh…

—Ada Goren

HEARTS TO SAY I LOVE YOU!

Here's a vocabulary-building song that's just right for the season.

(sung to the tune of "Skip to My Lou")

<u>(Red hearts, pink hearts, white hearts)</u>, too.
<u>(Red hearts, pink hearts, white hearts)</u>, too.
<u>(Red hearts, pink hearts, white hearts)</u>, too.
Hearts to say I love you!

<u>(Lace hearts, chocolate hearts, candy hearts)</u>, too.
<u>(Lace hearts, chocolate hearts, candy hearts)</u>, too.
<u>(Lace hearts, chocolate hearts, candy hearts)</u>, too.
Hearts to say I love you!

Repeat the song, substituting child-generated attributes for those in the blanks.

—Susan DeRiso

A VALENTINE FOR ME

(sung to the tune of "My Bonnie Lies Over the Ocean")

The mail truck is heading down my street.
I hope there'll be something for me!
It's Valentine's Day and I'm hoping
A valentine's coming for me!

Please have, please have
A valentine in there for me, for me.
Please have, please have
A valentine in there for me!

V-A-L-E-N-T-I-N-E

(sung to the tune of "Jingle Bells")

V-A-L-E-N-T-I-N-E
That's the way to spell valentine,
The special one for me, oh!
V-A-L-E-N-T-I-N-E
That's the way to spell valentine.
I hope there's one for me!

MUST BE VALENTINE!

(sung to the tune of "Must Be Santa")

Class: Who will be your valentine?
Teacher-chosen child: (Jesse) will be my valentine.
Class sings to (Jesse): Who will be your valentine?
(Jesse): (Carrie) will be my valentine.
Class: Valentine. Will be mine. Must be Carrie. Must be Jesse. Must be valen—valentines.

Continue singing the song, adding on all your students' names by repeating the "Must be (blank)" phrase (for example, "Valentine. Will be mine. Must be Carrie. Must be Jesse. Must be David. Must be Brandon. Must be Taylor. Must be Carley. Must be valen—valentines!"). If you need another phrase to end at the right part in the melody, add your own name to the list!

100TH DAY

(sung to the tune of "A-Tisket A-Tasket")

100! 100!
We've made it to 100!
We've been in school 100 days,
And we're so proud to be here!
We're proud! Say it loud!
We're so proud to be here!
We've been in school 100 days.
We've made it to 100!

—Ada Goren

100 DAYS, BY TENS

(sung to the tune of "Ten Little Indians")

10 little, 20 little, 30 little school days,
40 little, 50 little, 60 little school days,
70 little, 80 little, 90 little school days,
100 days, HOORAY!

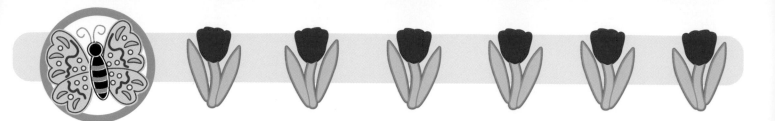

M-A-R-C-H

With this song, your little ones will always remember how to spell the month of March—guaranteed!

(sung to the tune of "The Hokey-Pokey")

It's M-A-R-C-H! It's M-A-R-C-H!
It's M-A-R-C-H and that spells the month of
   March!
Coming in like a lion, going out like a lamb,
That's M-A-R-C-H!

LION AND LAMB

(sung to the tune of "I Saw Three Ships")

When the weather's cold and windy, and
   windy, and windy,
When the weather's cold and windy,
We say it's like a lion.
Spoken: Roar!

When the weather's warm and sunny, and
   sunny, and sunny,
When the weather's warm and sunny,
We say it's like a lamb.
Spoken: Baa!

WINDY DAY FUN

The context is fun, and the skills are movement and vocabulary. What more could you ask for in a song?

(sung to the tune of "Rise and Shine")

I'll (run) with my kite and go flying, flying, flying.
I'll (run) with my kite and go flying, flying, flying.
I will (run) with my kite and go flying, flying, flying,
On a windy day.

Repeat the song, substituting a different action word in the blank each time. Suggested action words include: walk, skip, hop, *and* jump.

KITE HEIGHTS

(sung to the tune of "Row, Row, Row Your Boat")

One, two, three, four, five—
I'm flying through the sky.
Six, seven, eight, nine, ten—
I'm coming back again.

One, two, three, four, five—
I'm flying up so high.
Six, seven, eight, nine, ten—
Down I come again!

I'M A LITTLE KITE

(sung to the tune of "I'm a Little Teapot")

I'm a little kite, just look at me,
Shaped like a diamond, as you can see.
I just love to fly up in the air.
Swoosh! The wind will take me there!

—Ada Goren

I'M A LITTLE SHAMROCK

(sung to the tune of "I'm a Little Teapot")

I'm a little shamrock with green leaves.
Three in all,
Won't you count them, please?
When you find me near along your way,
Good luck I bring on St. Pat's Day!

—Lucia Kemp Henry

ARE YOU WEARING GREEN TODAY?

(sung to the tune of "The Muffin Man")

Are you wearing green today, green today, green today?
Are you wearing green today for St. Patrick's Day?

If your (shirt is) green today, green today, green today,
If your (shirt is) green today, please stand up!

Repeat the second stanza, having children substitute a different article of clothing each time.

—Deborah Carter

RAINBOW, RAINBOW

(sung to the tune of "Twinkle, Twinkle, Little Star)

Rainbow, rainbow, in the sky,
Full of colors—my, oh my!
Red and orange and yellow, too,
Green and blue and purple—ooh!
Rainbow, rainbow, in the sky,
Full of colors—my, oh my!

—Ada Goren

WEE LEPRECHAUNS

(sung to the tune of "The Mulberry Bush")

Wee leprechauns play hide-and-seek,
Hide-and-seek, hide-and-seek.
Wee leprechauns play hide-and-seek
On St. Patrick's Day!

Wee leprechauns guard pots of gold,
Pots of gold, pots of gold.
Wee leprechauns guard pots of gold
On St. Patrick's Day!

Wee leprechauns dance Irish jigs,
Irish jigs, Irish jigs.
Wee leprechauns dance Irish jigs
On St. Patrick's Day!

Wee leprechauns bring lots of luck,
Lots of luck, lots of luck.
Wee leprechauns bring lots of luck
On St. Patrick's Day!

—Deborah Carter

DO YOU KNOW WHY?

Little ones will be *delighted* to share these words of wisdom with their family members and friends—just in case someone doesn't know!

(sung to the tune of "The Muffin Man")

Do you know why I'm wearing green,
Wearing green, wearing green?
Do you know why I'm wearing green?
Today's St. Patrick's Day!

—Suzanne Moore

DANCING LEPRECHAUNS

This song provides the script for a fanciful performance. Or you could just sing and act it out impromptu for St. Patrick's Day fun!

(sung to the tune of "Six Little Ducks")

Little leprechauns that I once knew
Danced in the shamrocks two by two.
First they (<u>twirled</u>) and then they hopped.
Then they quickly sat when the music
   stopped, music stopped.
Then they quickly sat when the music
   stopped.

Repeat the song, substituting a different action word in the blank each time. Suggested action words include skipped, jogged, galloped, jumped, shuffled, *and* swayed.

—Deborah Carter

LUCKY LEPRECHAUN

(sung to the tune of "The Itsy-Bitsy Spider")

A lucky little leprechaun
Hid behind a tree.
When I smiled at him,
He smiled back at me.
He tipped his little green hat,
Then pointed way up high.
And a rainbow glowing brightly
Flew across the sky!

—Deborah Garmon

LEPRECHAUN STORY

(sung to the tune of "Jingle Bells")

Verse:
I saw a leprechaun
In green from head to toe.
And he went dancing by,
But, oh, where did he go?
He had a big black pot
All filled with shiny gold.
He took it to the rainbow's end,
And so the story goes!

Chorus:
Leprechaun, leprechaun,
Please come back our way!
We'd like to see you once again
On this St. Patrick's Day!
Leprechaun, leprechaun,
Please come back our way.
We'd like to see you once again
On this St. Patrick's Day!

—Ada Goren

RAINBOW COLORS

(sung to the tune of "London Bridge")

Rainbows spread across the sky
Painting colors way up high—
Red and orange, yellow, too,
Green, blue, and purple.

—Deborah Garmon

THE MAKING OF A RAINBOW

(sung to the tune of "Are You Sleeping?")

First the rain comes.
First the rain comes.
Then the sun.
Then the sun.
Next, a pretty rainbow.
Next, a pretty rainbow.
Oh, what fun!
Oh, what fun!

—Susan DeRiso

SPARKLE, SPARKLE POT OF GOLD

(sung to the tune of "Twinkle, Twinkle, Little Star")

Sparkle, sparkle pot of gold,
Leprechaun's secret must be told.
Follow the rainbow through the sky
To the end where shamrocks lie.
With some luck, I'll get to hold
That sparkle, sparkle pot of gold!

—Vicki Dabrowka

I'VE BEEN LOOKING FOR A RAINBOW

(sung to the tune of "I've Been Working on the Railroad")

I've been looking for a rainbow
On St. Patrick's Day.
I've been looking for a rainbow
On this Irish holiday.
For at the end of a rainbow,
Is a pot of gold, you see!
So I've been looking for a rainbow—
That pot of gold's for me!

—Suzanne Moore

IN THE SPRINGTIME

(sung to the tune of "Mary Had a Little Lamb")

(<u>Sway your arms</u>) in the springtime,
  the springtime, the springtime.
(<u>Sway your arms</u>) in the springtime,
  a happy time of year!

(<u>Wiggle your toes</u>) in the springtime,
  the springtime, the springtime.
(<u>Wiggle your toes</u>) in the springtime,
  a happy time of year!

(<u>Shrug your shoulders</u>) in the springtime,
  the springtime, the springtime.
(<u>Shrug your shoulders</u>) in the springtime,
  a happy time of year!

Now make up some verses of your own!

—Julie Granchelli

I'M A LITTLE ROBIN

(sung to the tune of "I'm a Little Teapot")

I'm a little robin flying round.
I build my nest with twigs I've found.
You can watch me pull worms from the ground
And listen for my sweet spring sound.

—Julie Granchelli

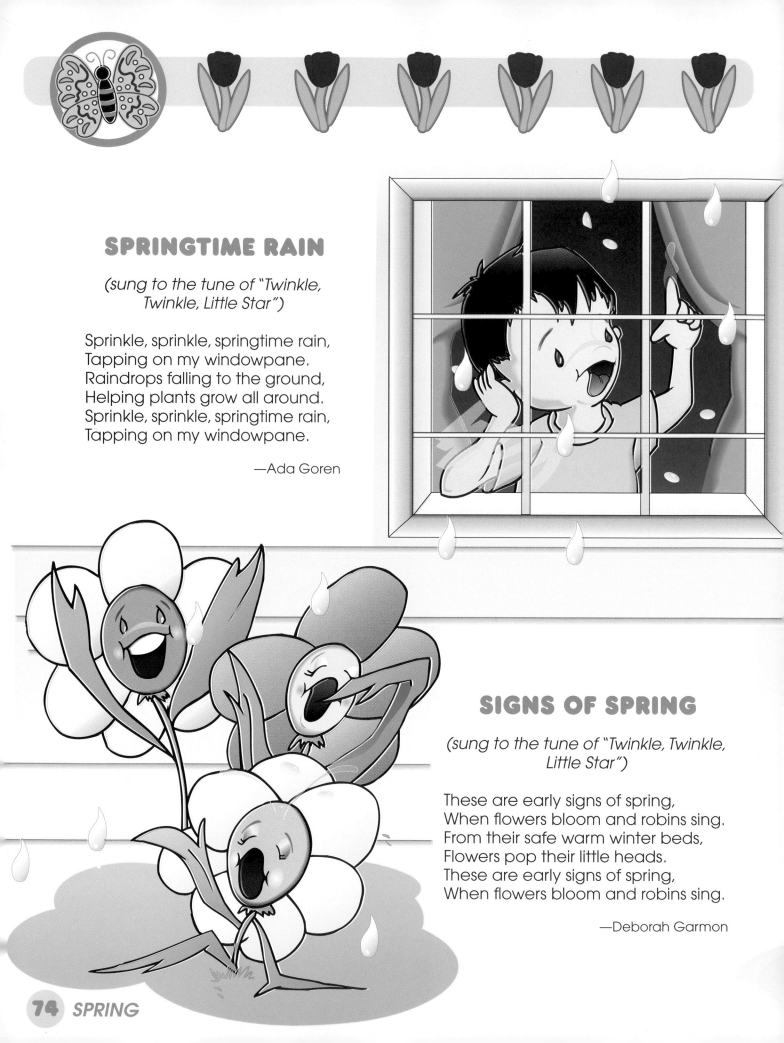

SPRINGTIME RAIN

(sung to the tune of "Twinkle, Twinkle, Little Star")

Sprinkle, sprinkle, springtime rain,
Tapping on my windowpane.
Raindrops falling to the ground,
Helping plants grow all around.
Sprinkle, sprinkle, springtime rain,
Tapping on my windowpane.

—Ada Goren

SIGNS OF SPRING

(sung to the tune of "Twinkle, Twinkle, Little Star")

These are early signs of spring,
When flowers bloom and robins sing.
From their safe warm winter beds,
Flowers pop their little heads.
These are early signs of spring,
When flowers bloom and robins sing.

—Deborah Garmon

MUDDY BUDDY

(sung to the tune of "Yankee Doodle")

The rain showers lasted yesterday,
And now my backyard's muddy.
Come slip and slide and play with me
And be my muddy buddy!

Muddy buddy, I can't wait!
Muddy buddy, hurry!
Come slip and slide and play with me
And be my muddy buddy!

—Donna Getzinger

DO THE RAINDROPS FALL?

Just as with the original lyrics ("Do Your Ears Hang Low?"), it's fun to speed up the tempo of this song a little bit each time you repeat it.

(sung to the tune of "Do Your Ears Hang Low?")

Do the raindrops fall?
Do they trickle? Do they plop?
Can you hear them on the roof—
Drizzle, drizzle, drop, drop.
Can you watch them on the window?
See them falling from the sky?
Do the raindrops fall?

—Donna Getzinger

RAIN

A little action poem with a lot of preschool science!

Here come the clouds,

And down falls the rain,

Falling on my roof

And my windowpane.

Gone are the clouds,

And gone is the rain.

Now the sun is shining brightly

On my windowpane.

—Deborah Garmon

PUDDLE BUILDING

(sung to the tune of "This Old Man")

From a cloud in the sky
Comes a sprinkle by-and-by.
With a drip-drop raindrops are falling one by one.
Puddle building's just begun!

—Colleen Dabney

THE RAIN IN THE SPRING

(sung to the tune of "The Wheels on the Bus")

The rain in the spring comes falling down,
Falling down, falling down.
The rain in the spring comes falling down
On all the (flowers).

Repeat the song and invite your children to fill in the blank by thinking of other things that get rained on, such as grass, people, trees, and ducks.

—Ada Goren

SPELLING IN THE SPRING

(sung to the tune of "Bingo")

In the spring the rain falls down.
Rainy is the weather.
R-A-I-N-Y
R-A-I-N-Y
R-A-I-N-Y
And rainy is the weather.

In the spring the sun shines round.
Sunny is the weather.
S-U-N-N-Y
S-U-N-N-Y
S-U-N-N-Y
And sunny is the weather.

In the spring the wind does blow.
Windy is the weather.
W-I-N-D-Y
W-I-N-D-Y
W-I-N-D-Y
And windy is the weather.

—Julie Granchelli

HAVE YOU EVER SEEN A RAIN CLOUD?

(sung to the tune of "Did You Ever See a Lassie?")

Have you ever seen a rain cloud,
A rain cloud, a rain cloud?
Have you ever seen a rain cloud
    rain this way and that?
Rain this way and that way,
And that way and this way?
Have you ever seen a rain cloud
    rain this way and that?

Have you ever seen the lightning,
The lightning, the lightning?
Have you ever seen the lightning
    flash this way and that?
Flash this way and that way,
And that way and this way?
Have you ever seen the lightning
    flash this way and that?

Have you ever heard the thunder,
The thunder, the thunder?
Have you ever heard the thunder
    boom this way and that?
Boom this way and that way,
And that way and this way?
Have you ever heard the thunder
    boom this way and that?

—Suzanne Moore

CRASH
BOOM

THE RAINBOW SONG

(sung to the tune of "I'm a Little Teapot")

Here comes a little rain cloud gray and black.
Raindrops fall—pit-a-pat, pit-a-pat.
Soon the sun comes out and what do you know?
High above is a big rainbow!

—Roxanne LaBell Dearman

DRIP-DROP RAINDROPS

(sung to the tune of "Twinkle, Twinkle, Little Star")

Drip-drop, drop-drip, raindrops fall.
One, two, three drops—raindrops all.
Falling from the clouds up high,
Little raindrops from the sky.
Drip-drop, drop-drip, raindrops fall.
One, two, three drops—raindrops all.

Extension:
• To introduce the term *precipitation*,
  substitute "Precipitation from the sky"
  for the fourth line of the song.

—Kimberly A. Minafo

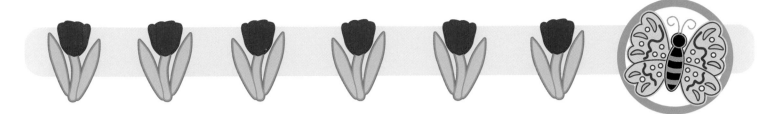

PUDDLES!

(sung to the tune of "Are You Sleeping?")

Rain is falling, rain is falling
From the sky, from the sky.
Raindrops making puddles.
Raindrops making puddles.
All around. All around.

Raindrop puddles, raindrop puddles
On the ground, on the ground.
Let's go puddle jumping!
Let's go puddle jumping!
All around. All around.

—Julie Granchelli

PUDDLE PROBLEMS

Your little ones will be able to relate to the predicament in these puddle problems!

(sung to the tune of "A-Tisket A-Tasket")

A-squishin' a-squashin'
My mom won't like the washin'.
She said stay in, but I went out,
And now my shoes are sloshin'!

I'm muddy and soaked through.
My sneakers once were brand-new.
I saw the puddle, meant to jump,
But somehow I went right through!

A-squishin' a-squashin'
My mom won't like the washin'.
She said stay in, but I went out,
And now my shoes are sloshin'!

—Kimberly A. Minafo

I LOVE TO RECYCLE

Use this song to help your students remember which materials can be recycled.

(sung to the tune of "For He's a Jolly Good Fellow")

I love to recycle (<u>plastic</u>).
I love to recycle (<u>plastic</u>).
I love to recycle (<u>plastic</u>)
To keep the earth so clean.
To keep the earth so clean,
To keep the earth so clean,
I love to recycle (<u>plastic</u>)
To keep the earth so clean!

Repeat the song, replacing the underlined word with other recycling options, such as glass, paper, and aluminum.

—Suzanne Moore

PLANET EARTH

(sung to the tune of "Bingo")

There is a planet we call home
And Earth is its name-o.
E-A-R-T-H
E-A-R-T-H
E-A-R-T-H
And Earth is its name-o!

HAPPY MAY DAY

This is a great little number to sing as a class when you deliver May Day treats to your school's principal, secretary, and other special people.

(sung to the tune of "Happy Birthday to You")

Happy May Day to you.
Happy May Day to you.
Happy May Day, dear (<u>person's name</u>).
Happy May Day to you.

—Julie Granchelli

MAY DAY!

(sung to the tune of "London Bridge")

Winter's gone, it's time for spring,
Time for spring, time for spring.
Winter's gone, it's time for spring.
May 1—May Day!

Robins sing, it's time for spring,
Time for spring, time for spring.
Robins sing, it's time for spring.
May 1—May Day!

Flowers bloom, it's time for spring,
Time for spring, time for spring.
Flowers bloom, it's time for spring.
May 1—May Day!

—Suzanne Moore

MAY DAY POEM
(poem)

It's the first day of May.

I hear birds sing everywhere.

Winter is over,

And spring is in the air.

Flowers are growing.

The sun is shining bright.

Little leaves peek

From every plant in sight.

I'll pick some garden flowers

And tie them with a string,

Then give them all to you

To celebrate spring!

—Lucia Kemp Henry

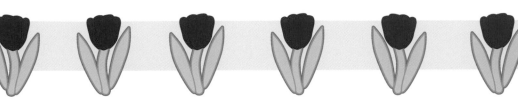

MOM, I LOVE YOU

(sung to the tune of
"Twinkle, Twinkle, Little Star")

Mom, I love you. I agree!
That you're the perfect mom for me.
When I'm sad or feeling blue,
You know just the thing to do.
As my mom you are so fine,
And I'm so glad that you are mine!

—Susan DeRiso

ON MOTHER'S DAY

(sung to the tune of
"The Mulberry Bush")

What will you do on Mother's Day,
Mother's Day, Mother's Day?
What will you do on Mother's Day,
All day long?

I'll (hug my mom) on Mother's Day,
Mother's Day, Mother's Day.
I'll (hug my mom) on Mother's Day,
All day long.

That's what I'll do on Mother's Day,
Mother's Day, Mother's Day.
That's what I'll do on Mother's Day,
All day long.

Sing the song again, replacing the
underlined words in the second
verse with children's ideas, such as
the phrases kiss my mom, thank my
mom, *and* give Mom a gift.

—Suzanne Moore

LOVE TO YOU ON MOTHER'S DAY

(sung to the tune of "I'm a Little Teapot")

You are the best mother
In the world!
And I am the luckiest boy or girl!
You take care of me in every way.
Love to you on Mother's Day!

This song could be used for Father's Day by substituting father *and* Father's Day *appropriately.*

—Ada Goren

M-O-M

(sung to the tune of "If You're Happy and You Know It")

If you love your M-O-M, blow her a kiss.
If you love your M-O-M, blow her a kiss.
If you love your M-O-M, tell her once and then again.
If you love your M-O-M, blow her a kiss.

If you love your M-O-M, give her a hug.
If you love your M-O-M, give her a hug.
If you love your M-O-M, tell her once and then again.
If you love your M-O-M, give her a hug.

If you love your M-O-M, say "I love you!"
If you love your M-O-M, say "I love you!"
If you love your M-O-M, tell her once and then again.
If you love your M-O-M, say "I love you!"

—Roxanne LaBell Dearman

TWO LITTLE EGGS
(poem)

Two little eggs

In a nest soft and deep.

Two eggs crack;

Then two birds peep!

Two birds eat,

And two birds sleep.

Then two fly away

With a "Cheep! Cheep! Cheep!"

—Lucia Kemp Henry

EASTER BUNNY

(sung to the tune of "Short'nin' Bread")

Easter Bunny's coming in the mornin', mornin'.
Easter Bunny's coming and I can't wait.
Easter Bunny's coming in the mornin', mornin'.
Easter Bunny's coming and I can't wait.
What will he bring me? What kind of treat?
Hope he brings (jelly beans) for me to eat.

Repeat the song, asking children to fill in the blank with a different suggestion each time.

—Lucia Kemp Henry

EASTERTIME

(sung to the tune of "Jingle Bells")

Eastertime is here,
A special time of year
That's filled with springtime joy
For every girl and boy.
Bunnies hop around
And chicks will "peep" their sound.
Oh, what fun it is to color Easter
    eggs tonight. Oh!

Eastertime! Eastertime!
A special time of year.
Oh, what fun it is to find
Easter baskets full of cheer!
Eastertime! Eastertime!
A special time of year.
Oh, what fun it is to find
Easter baskets full of cheer!

—Deborah Garmon

EASTER FUN
(Poem)

Here comes the Easter Bunny

Hopping down the trail,

Wiggling his bunny ears,

Wiggling his tail.

Hurry, Mr. Easter Bunny!

Deliver all your eggs!

Then hop away down the bunny trail on

Your Easter Bunny legs.

—Deborah Garmon

BABY CHICKS

(sung to the tune of
"Twinkle, Twinkle, Little Star")

Baby chicks hatch from eggs.
They wiggle their wings
And shake their legs.
Once they're out of their egg homes,
They are free to peep and roam.
Baby chicks hatch from eggs.
They wiggle their wings
And shake their legs.

—Betsy Gaynor

OUT IN THE MEADOW

*(sung to the tune of
"Up on the Housetop")*

Out in the meadow Bunny hops,
Gathering eggs and lollipops,
Filling baskets, hip hooray!
Getting ready for Easter Day.
Hop, hop, hop! Please don't stop!
Hop, hop, hop! Please don't stop!
Filling baskets, hip hooray!
Getting ready for Easter Day.

—Suzanne Moore

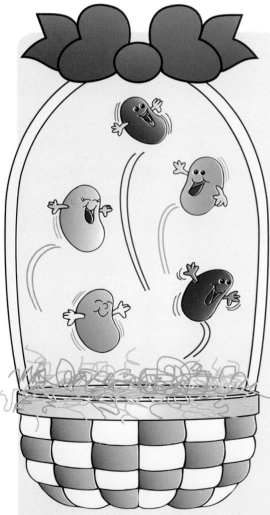

FIVE LITTLE JELLY BEANS

Here's a great little counting song to use with jelly bean cutouts or even real ones. Have fun!

(sung to the tune of "Five Little Speckled Frogs")

(Five) little jelly beans—
Prettiest I've ever seen!
All in my Easter basket—yum! *(spoken: "Mmm-mmm!")*
I'll take one out to eat.
Oh, what an Easter treat!
Now there are (four) little jelly beans. *(spoken: "Oh boy!")*

Continue singing the song, counting down by replacing the number words in the first and last lines of the song appropriately. Then conclude with the last verse.

One little jelly bean—
Prettiest I've ever seen!
It's in my Easter basket—yum! *(spoken: "Mmm-mmm!")*
I'll take it out to eat;
Oh, what an Easter treat!
Now there are no little jelly beans. *(spoken: "Oh no!")*

—Ada Goren

FLOWERS GROW

(sung to the tune of "Down By the Station")

Down in the dark earth,
Early in the springtime,
See the little sprouts
Start poking through the ground.

See the stems a-growing!
See the leaves unfolding!
Up, up, up, up—
Flowers grow!

—Ada Goren

PLANTING

(sung to the tune of "Head, Shoulders, Knees, and Toes")

Poke a hole right in the ground,
In the ground.
Put a seed in—pat it down,
Pat it down.
With earth on top,
You water drop by drop.
Then warm sun shines down all around,
All around!

—Linda Gordetsky

COLORFUL FLOWERS

Make ten laminated construction paper cutouts, one to go with each flower color you'd like to sing about in this song. Just right for beginning counters and color learners!

(sung to the tune of "Ten Little Indians")

One (<u>red</u>), two (<u>red</u>), three (<u>red</u>) flowers,
Four (<u>red</u>), five (<u>red</u>), six (<u>red</u>) flowers,
Seven (<u>red</u>), eight (<u>red</u>), nine (<u>red</u>) flowers.
Ten (<u>red</u>) flowers are growing.

—Julie Granchelli

IS YOUR GARDEN FULL OF FLOWERS?

(sung to the tune of "If You're Happy and You Know It")

Is your garden full of flowers just like mine?
Is your garden full of flowers just like mine?
<u>(I have roses bright and red
Growing in my flower bed.)</u>
Is your garden full of flowers just like mine?

Encourage your children to think of other types of flowers and rhyming phrases for additional verses of this song. Examples: I have daisies yellow and white growing in the bright sunlight. I have sunflowers yellow and green—the tallest I've ever seen!

—Deborah Garmon

MARY PLANTS A FLOWER SEED

(sung to the tune of "Mary Had a Little Lamb")

Mary plants a flower seed,
Flower seed, flower seed.
Mary plants a flower seed
In her garden in the spring.

Sun and water help it grow,
Help it grow, help it grow.
Sun and water help it grow
In her garden in the spring.

Mary picks her pretty flower,
Pretty flower, pretty flower.
Mary picks her pretty flower
And gives it to her favorite friend.

—Julie Granchelli

I CAN PLANT SOME LITTLE SEEDS

(sung to the tune of "If You're Happy and You Know It")

I can plant some (little) seeds in the ground.
I can plant some (little) seeds in the ground.
I can plant some (little) seeds; sun and water's
     what they need.
I can plant some (little) seeds in the ground.

With some water and some sun, the seeds will grow.
With some water and some sun, the seeds will grow.
They will grow, they will grow; leaves above and
     roots below.
With some water and some sun, the seeds will grow.

Sing new verses, replacing the underlined word with child-generated names of seeds such as pumpkin *and* apple.

—Suzanne Moore

HOW FLOWERS GROW

(sung to the tune of "The Muffin Man")

Do you know how flowers grow,
Flowers grow? Flowers grow?
Do you know how flowers grow?
I will tell you now!

First you plant a flower seed,
A flower seed, a flower seed.
First you plant a flower seed
And cover it with soil.

Then you gently water it,
Water it, water it.
Then you gently water it
And roots begin to grow.

Then the sprout pops through the ground,
Through the ground, through the ground.
Then the sprout pops through the ground
And grows so leafy green.

Sun and water help it grow,
Help it grow, help it grow.
Sun and water help it grow
And bloom into a flower.

—Michelle McCormick

CHOOSING ONE?

(sung to the tune of "Six Little Ducks")

Flowers bloom in the springtime sun.
How can I choose to pick just one?
With so many flowers, what shall I do?
I'll pick a whole bouquet,
Then give it to you, give it to you!
I'll pick a whole bouquet, then give it to you!

—Suzanne Moore

CATERPILLAR SONG

(sung to the tune of "I'm a Little Teapot")

I'm a little caterpillar
Small and shy.
I'll build a cocoon
Where I can hide.
When I come back out
To your surprise,
I'll be a lovely butterfly!

—Eva Bareis

CATERPILLAR'S CRAWLING

Your little ones will get a kick out of performing this slippery little caterpillar song.

(sung to the tune of "Head, Shoulders, Knees, and Toes")

Caterpillar's on my nose, on my nose.
Crawling to my shoulder—
Oops! He's on my toes!
Now he's crawling back up to my knees.
Now Caterpillar's on my head, if you please!

—Betty Silkunas

CATERPILLAR

(sung to the tune of "Kookaburra")

Caterpillar crawls in the leafy tree,
Eating all the leaves that he can see.
Grow, caterpillar! Grow, caterpillar!
What will you soon be?

Caterpillar spins in the leafy tree,
Spinning a cocoon snug as can be.
Rest, caterpillar! Rest, caterpillar!
What will you soon be?

Butterfly starts to wiggle free,
Leaving that cocoon snug as can be.
Fly, butterfly! Fly, butterfly!
What a change to see!

—Ada Goren

SING A SONG OF BUTTERFLIES

(sung to the tune of "Sing a Song of Sixpence")

Sing a song of butterflies—
Yellow, red, and blue.
Breaking from their pupas,
Their wings are wet and new.
Next, their wings are drying
And flapping in the sun.
Then off they fly for nectar;
The fun has just begun!

—Suzanne Moore

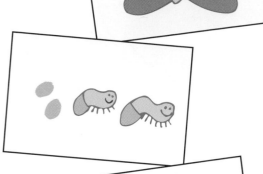

BUTTERFLY LIFE

(sung to the tune of "The Mulberry Bush")

It's time to start watching butterflies grow,
Butterflies grow, butterflies grow.
It's time to start watching butterflies grow
So early in the springtime.

The caterpillars hatch from eggs,
Hatch from eggs, hatch from eggs.
The caterpillars hatch from eggs
So early in the springtime.

The caterpillar eats and grows,
Eats and grows, eats and grows.
The caterpillar eats and grows
So early in the springtime.

It turns into a chrysalis,
A chrysalis, a chrysalis.
It turns into a chrysalis
So early in the springtime.

A new butterfly comes out of the case,
Out of the case, out of the case.
A new butterfly comes out of the case
So early in the springtime.

The wings begin to pump and dry,
Pump and dry, pump and dry.
The wings begin to pump and dry
So early in the springtime.

The new butterfly then flies away,
Flies away, flies away.
The new butterfly then flies away
So early in the springtime.

—Kim Minafo

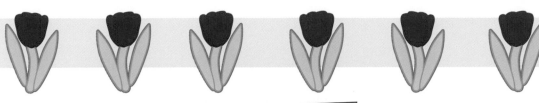

A BUTTERFLY STORY

This little story-poem is a great one to make into a child-illustrated class book!

I spied a little caterpillar crawling across the land.
His furry body quivered as I touched him with my hand.

His coat was quite magnificent, striped with black and yellow.
His tiny feet were many—a wiggly sort of fellow!

I watched a little longer, and he soon grew used to me.
Then he turned on stumpy legs and headed up a tree.

He found a little niche carved right into the bark.
Safe and sound, he curled right up and stayed there until dark.

When morning came the very next day, I hurried to that spot.
But no caterpillar greeted me, just a little "knot."

My friend had gone and left instead a little brown cocoon.
But I wasn't sad, for in my heart, I knew I'd see him soon.

Winter passed; the days grew warm; I watched his little nest.
And I began to wonder if he would wake up from his rest.

At last one sunny morning, the shell lay broken wide.
Its owner, now with drying wings, fluttered on the side.

Proud and smart it waited, then launched off for the sky.
No longer a little caterpillar, but a beautiful butterfly!

—Michelle McCormick

I'M A FROG

(sung to the tune of "I'm a Nut")

I'm a frog. I live in a pond.
Of tasty flies I'm very fond.
I like to swim; I like to hop.
Hear me croak; I never stop!

I'm a frog!
I'm a frog!
I'm a big green frog!

—Ada Goren

GUESS WHO'S IN THE POND

As you sing this song, ask children to fill in the blank at the end of each verse. For younger children, you might want to have them choose from the animals shown in the illustration.

(sung to the tune of "The Muffin Man")

Guess who's on the lily pad,
The lily pad, the lily pad.
Guess who's on the lily pad.
It must be (a frog).

Guess who's swimming underwater,
Underwater, underwater.
Guess who's swimming underwater.
It must be (a fish).

Guess who's working on a dam,
On a dam, on a dam.
Guess who's working on a dam.
It must be (a beaver).

Guess who's waddling to the pond,
To the pond, to the pond.
Guess who's waddling to the pond.
It must be (a duck).

—Donna Getzinger

IN THE POND NOW

When you sing this song, seat your youngsters in a circle that represents a pond. As each new character is introduced in the song, select a child (or children) to go to the middle of the pond and act out the part. Have each character stay in the pond until the snake is introduced. At that point, instinct takes over!

(sung to the tune of "There's a Hole in the Bucket")

There's a frog in the pond,
In the pond, in the pond now.
There's a frog in the pond now,
A frog in the pond!

There are two fish in the pond,
In the pond, in the pond now.
There are two fish in the pond now,
Two fish in the pond!

There are three turtles in the pond,
In the pond, in the pond now.
There are three turtles in the pond now,
Three turtles in the pond!

There are four ducks in the pond,
In the pond, in the pond now.
There are four ducks in the pond now,
Four ducks in the pond!

There are five snails in the pond,
In the pond, in the pond now.
There are five snails in the pond now,
Five snails in the pond!

There's…a…sssssssnake in the pond,
In the pond, in the pond now.
There's a sssssssnake in the pond now,
And he's all alone!

—Colleen Dabney

I LOOK IN THE POND

(sung to the tune of "Skip to My Lou")

I look in the pond and what do I see?
I look in the pond and what do I see?
I look in the pond and what do I see?
A (turtle) smiling back at me.

Repeat the song, asking children to fill in the blank with a new pond animal each time. Suggestions include big fish, green frog, tadpole, white duck, and beaver.

—Suzanne Moore

WHO GOES SWIMMING IN THE POND?

(sung to the tune of "Old MacDonald Had a Farm")

Who goes swimming in the pond
On a warm spring day?
(Frog) goes swimming in the pond
Where he likes to play.
With a splish-splash here and a splish-splash there.
Here a splish, there a splash,
Everywhere a splish-splash.
(Frog) goes swimming in the pond
On a warm spring day.

Repeat the song, asking children to fill in the blank with a new pond animal each time. Suggestions include fish, duck, turtle, and snake.

—Lucia Kemp Henry

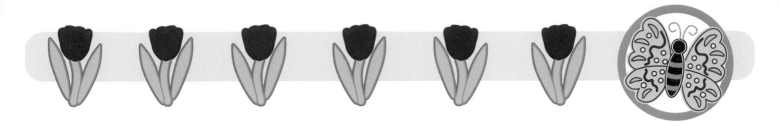

WIGGLE-WAGGLE WONDERS

(sung to the tune of "When the Saints Go Marching In")

Oh, tadpoles hatch from little eggs.
Oh, tadpoles hatch from little eggs.
And their tails go wiggle-waggle
When tadpoles hatch from little eggs.

And tadpoles swim around the pond.
And tadpoles swim around the pond.
And their tails go wiggle-waggle
When tadpoles swim around the pond.

And then their legs begin to grow.
And then their legs begin to grow.
And their tails go wiggle-waggle
When their legs begin to grow.

And then the tail soon disappears.
And then the tail soon disappears.
And it can't go wiggle-waggle
When the tail soon disappears.

But when the frog jumps in the pond,
But when the frog jumps in the pond,
Oh, the water wiggle-waggles
When the frog jumps in the pond!

—Suzanne Moore

THE DUCKY-POKEY

(sung to the tune of "The Hokey-Pokey")

You put your (<u>right wing</u>) in.
You put your (<u>right wing</u>) out.
You put your (<u>right wing</u>) in and you shake it all about.
You do the ducky-pokey and you waddle yourself around.
That's what it's all about! Quack! Quack!

*Repeat the song, substituting the following duck body
parts for the underlined word or words each time:* left wing,
duck bill, tail feathers, *and* webbed feet.

—Ada Goren

A FROG'S LIFE

Setting science in a song is a surefire way to learn the facts!

(sung to the tune of "Where Is Thumbkin?")

How does a frog grow?
How does a frog grow?
The mama lays the eggs.
The mama lays the eggs.
She lays them in the water
Right there where she oughtta.
Mama lays the eggs. Mama lays the eggs.

Then the eggs hatch.
Then the eggs hatch.
Out come tadpoles.
Out come tadpoles.
Swimming in the water
Right there where they oughtta.
Tadpoles swim. Tadpoles swim.

Then the legs grow,
Then the legs grow,
On the tadpole.
On the tadpole.
Still swimming in the water
Right there where he oughtta.
Tadpole swims. Tadpole swims.

Tadpole grows up.
Tadpole grows up.
The tail disappears.
The tail disappears.
Still swimming in the water
Right there where he oughtta.
Now he's a frog! Now he's a frog!

—adapted from an idea by Vicki Dabrowka

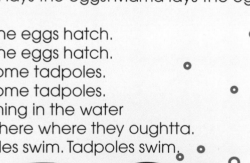

JOBS ON THE FARM

As your youngsters sing this song, encourage them to make up motions and sound effects for each new action. There's a lot to do, it's true!

(sung to the tune of "If You're Happy and You Know It")

If you want to be a farmer
(Milk the cows).
If you want to be a farmer
(Milk the cows).
There's a lot to do, it's true
And that's what farmers do.
If you want to be a farmer
(Milk the cows).

Repeat the song, substituting other farm jobs—such as feed the pigs, gather the eggs, plant the seeds, pick the corn, and drive the tractor—for the underlined words.

—Ada Goren

HUSH, LITTLE CALF

(sung to the tune of "Hush, Little Baby")

Hush, little (calf) now don't you cry.
Mama (cow) will sing you a lullaby.
She'll (moo, moo, moo) to have you near.
So hush, little (calf), Mama (cow) is here.

Repeat the song, replacing the underlined words with new ones each time.
Examples: lamb/sheep/baa, baa, baa; foal/horse/neigh, neigh, neigh; piglet/pig/oink, oink, oink.

—Lucia Kemp Henry

SONGS ON THE FARM

(sung to the tune of "The Wheels on the Bus")

The (<u>rooster</u>) on the farm says (<u>cock-a-doodle-doo</u>),
(<u>Cock-a-doodle-doo, cock-a-doodle-doo</u>).
The (<u>rooster</u>) on the farm says (<u>cock-a-doodle-doo</u>),
All the livelong day.

Repeat the song, substituting other farm animals and sounds each time.

—Ada Goren

cock-a-doodle-doo

NAMING BABY

(sung to the tune of "The Muffin Man")

What do we call a baby (<u>pig</u>),
A baby (<u>pig</u>), a baby (<u>pig</u>)?
What do we call a baby (<u>pig</u>)?
It's called a (<u>piglet</u>)!

Repeat the song, substituting other animal names for the underlined words.

—Ada Goren

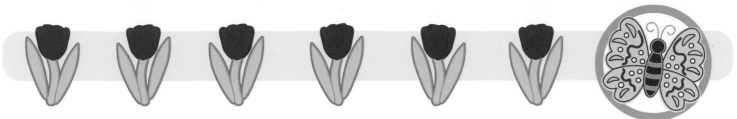

FARM WORK

(sung to the tune of "The Wheels on the Bus")

The farmer drives his truck from field to field,
Field to field, field to field.
The farmer drives his truck from field to field,
Down on the farm.

The hen on the farm sits on her nest,
On her nest, on her nest.
The hen on the farm sits on her nest,
Down on the farm.

The cow on the farm gives lots of milk,
Lots of milk, lots of milk.
The cow on the farm gives lots of milk,
Down on the farm.

The children on the farm have chores to do,
Chores to do, chores to do.
The children on the farm have chores to do,
Down on the farm.

Encourage your students to generate and sing additional verses to this song.

—Kimberly A. Minafo

SQUISHY-WISHY MUD

(sung to the tune of "The Muffin Man")

Oh, did you know the (little pink pig),
The (little pink pig, the little pink pig).
Oh, did you know the (little pink pig)
Turned brown in the squishy-wishy mud?

Continue singing the song, substituting a different animal and its color each time.

Examples:
little green frog
little white duck
little red hen
little gray cat

—Roxanne LaBell Dearman

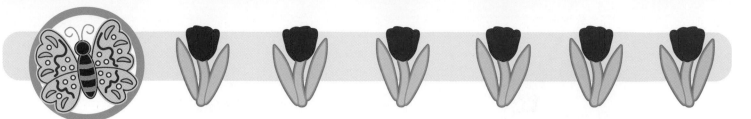

MOVE ME ON UP!

(sung to the tune of "Take Me Out to the Ballgame")

Move me on up to the first grade.
I have worked very hard.
I know my letters and numbers, too.
I follow directions and tie my own shoes.
So please move me on up to the first grade.
I want to learn even more!
So it's time I'm movin' along
Let first grade begin!

—Kimberly A. Minafo

NEXT YEAR!

(sung to the tune of "Santa Claus Is Coming to Town")

I've learned a whole lot.

I'm much bigger now.

I know how to listen

And do things—oh, wow!

I'm going to (kindergarten) next year!

—Ada Goren

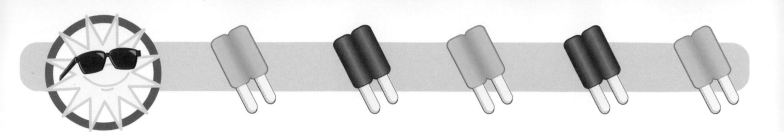

INSECT BODY PARTS

(sung to the tune of "Camptown Races")

An insect has three body parts.
Count 'em, three parts.
An insect has three body parts
All the livelong day.
It has to have a head
And a thorax, too.
Last, it has an abdomen.
Three body parts, it's true!

—Suzanne Moore

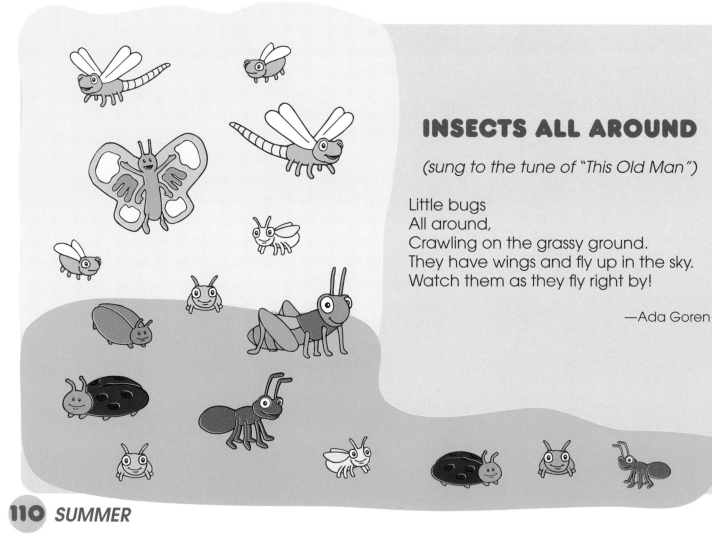

INSECTS ALL AROUND

(sung to the tune of "This Old Man")

Little bugs
All around,
Crawling on the grassy ground.
They have wings and fly up in the sky.
Watch them as they fly right by!

—Ada Goren

GRASSHOPPER ESCAPE

(sung to the tune of "Are You Sleeping?")

You can't catch me.
You can't catch me.
I'm too quick!
I'm too quick!
Hopping leaf to leaf now.
It is my belief now—
I'm too quick!
I'm too quick!

—Betty Silkunas

FIVE BIG GRASSHOPPERS
(poem)

Five big grasshoppers
On a little twig.
The first one said, "I feel a little big."
The second one said, "I need a bit more space."
The third one said, "You're standing in my place!"
The fourth one said, "I feel like I might fall."
The fifth one said, "There's just not room for all."
So they wiggled and they wobbled and they started to sway.
Then the five big grasshoppers hopped far away!

—Lucia Kemp Henry

FIREFLY NIGHT

(sung to the tune of "Are You Sleeping?")

Firefly, firefly,
Small and bright,
Small and bright,
I can see you glowing,
I can see you glowing,
In the night.
In the night.

—Eva Bareis

FIREFLIES, WON'T YOU COME OUT TONIGHT?

(sung to the tune of "Buffalo Gals")

Fireflies, won't you come out tonight,
Come out tonight, come out tonight?
Fireflies, won't you come out tonight
And fly by the light of the moon?

Fireflies, won't you turn on your lights,
Turn on your lights, turn on your lights?
Fireflies, won't you turn on your lights
And light up the summer night?

—Suzanne Moore

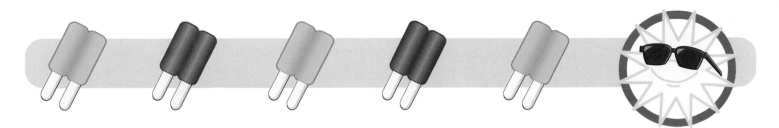

TEN LITTLE FIREFLIES

(sung to the tune of "Six Little Ducks")

(Ten) little fireflies in the night
Twinkle and blink, what a beautiful sight.
But one firefly with a pretty little wink
Flew away from the others with a blink, blink, blink.
Blink, blink, blink.
Flew away from the others with a blink, blink, blink.

Repeat the song, counting down by one each time.

One little firefly in the night
Twinkles and blinks, what a beautiful sight.
And that one firefly with a pretty little wink
Twinkled all alone with a blink, blink, blink.
Blink, blink, blink.
Twinkled all alone with a blink, blink, blink.

—Lucia Kemp Henry

FLASHING FIREFLY

(sung to the tune of "Twinkle, Twinkle, Little Star")

Flashing, flashing in the night
See the firefly's glowing light!
Flashing high and flashing low,
Flashing fast and flashing slow.
Flashing, flashing in the night,
See the firefly's glowing light!

—Roxanne LaBell Dearman

FIREFLY, I SEE YOUR LIGHT!

(sung to the tune of "Shoo Fly")

Firefly, I see your light!
Firefly, I see your light!
Firefly, I see your light!
I see you shine on summer nights!

—Ada Goren

FIREFLIES ARE OUT TONIGHT

(sung to the tune of "The Muffin Man")

Do you see a flash of light,
A flash of light, a flash of light?
Do you see a flash of light?
Are fireflies out tonight?

Yes, I see a flash of light,
A flash of light, a flash of light.
Yes, I see a flash of light.
Fireflies are out tonight!

—Betty Silkunas

INSECTS!

(sung to the tune of "A Ring o' Roses")

Look at all the insects.
They look like little moving specks.
Crawling, flying,
Off they go!

Buzzing Mr. Bumblebee
Flies to all the flowers he sees—
Daffodil, lilac bush,
Geranium!

Mosquito wants to bite you.
Lands upon your little shoe.
Raise your hand, shoo him off.
Get out of here!

Firefly is a bright one.
Firefly has a light on.
Watch his light flick on and off
Through the night!

Grasshopper jumps a long way.
Escapes a hungry blue jay.
First he's here, then he's there,
Hopping all the way!

Ladybug has black spots.
Count the little black dots.
Farmer likes Miss Ladybug
For all the bugs she eats!

Look at all the insects.
They look like little moving specks.
Crawling, flying,
Off they go!

—Michelle McCormick

I'M A LITTLE INSECT

(sung to the tune of "I'm a Little Teapot")

I'm a little insect.
What's my name?
Nibbling picnic lunches is my game.
If you should leave your food out,
I will know.
And I'll nibble, nibble, nibble,
Then off I'll go!

—Betty Silkunas

DOWN BY THE ANTHILL

Here's an insect-related song that mixes math into the fun! Try it!

(sung to the tune of "Down By the Station")

Down by the anthill early in the morning,
Ants go marching (<u>one by one</u>) all in a row.
See the little leader turn to tell the others,
"One, two, three, four! Hup, let's go!"

Repeat the song, substituting the phrases two by two *and* three by three *in the blank. As students sing the different verses, have them line up according to the numbers indicated. If abilities permit, keep going!*

—Lucia Kemp Henry

I'VE GOT THE BEST FATHER

(sung to the tune of "He's Got the Whole World in His Hands")

I've got the best father in the world!
I've got the best father in the world!
I've got the best father in the world!
I'm the luckiest boy or girl!

—Ada Goren

FATHER'S DAY

(sung to the tune of "Pop! Goes the Weasel")

Father's Day comes once a year.
It's when we celebrate
The love we have for all our dads.
Fathers are great!

—Deborah Garmon

ON FATHER'S DAY

(sung to the tune of "A Frog Went A-Courtin'")

Gonna (hug) my dad on Father's Day, uh-huh.
Gonna (hug) my dad on Father's Day, uh-huh.
Gonna (hug) my dad on Father's Day
And show him that I love him in a special way,
Uh-huh, oh yeah, uh-huh.

Repeat the song, encouraging children to replace the underlined words with other words such as thank, kiss, *and* help.

—Suzanne Moore

THE FOURTH OF JULY

(sung to the tune of "The Wheels on the Bus")

The Fourth of July is lots of fun, lots of fun, lots of fun.
Flags wave high; parades go by—
The Fourth of July!

The Fourth of July is lots of fun, lots of fun, lots of fun.
Fireworks boom and sparkle, too—
The Fourth of July!

The Fourth of July is lots of fun, lots of fun, lots of fun.
We love you, red, white, and blue—
The Fourth of July!

—Deborah Garmon

IT'S INDEPENDENCE DAY!

(sung to the tune of "London Bridge")

See the fireworks light the sky,
Light the sky, light the sky.
See the fireworks light the sky.
It's Independence Day!

See the flag fly high and proud,
High and proud, high and proud.
See the flag fly high and proud.
It's Independence Day!

Lift your voices; sing aloud,
Sing aloud, sing aloud.
Lift your voices; sing aloud.
It's Independence Day!

—Colleen Dabney

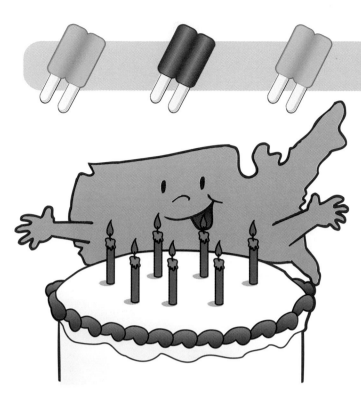

HAPPY BIRTHDAY, AMERICA!

(sung to the tune of "Happy Birthday to You")

Happy birthday to you,
To the red, white, and blue.
Stars and Stripes fly forever.
America, we love you!

—Kimberly A. Minafo

RED, WHITE, AND BLUE,
WE LOVE YOU!

(sung to the tune of "Jingle Bells")

Red, white, and blue
We love you.
It's Independence Day!
Stars and Stripes, we love you, too.
Happy birthday, USA!

(Repeat)

—Roxanne LaBell Dearman

INDEPENDENCE DAY

(sung to the tune of "Ta Ra Ra Boom De Ay")

It's Independence Day!
Let's shout a big hooray!
We wave our flags all day,
Parading all the way.

We march a-one, a-two
Along the avenue.
It's fun for me and you.
Hooray, red, white, and blue!

—Lucia Kemp Henry

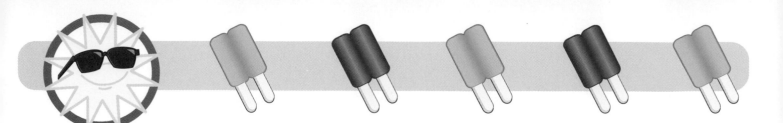

LET'S GO ON A PICNIC

(sung to the tune of "Mary Wore Her Red Dress")

Let's go on a picnic, picnic, picnic.
Let's go on a picnic. What will you pack?

I will pack (<u>a sandwich, a sandwich, a sandwich</u>).
I will pack (<u>a sandwich</u>). That's what I'll pack!

*Sing the song again, replacing the underlined
words with other picnic words, such as* potato
chips, a watermelon, an apple, *and* a cold drink.

—Suzanne Moore

OH, PICNIC LUNCH

(sung to the tune of "O Christmas Tree")

O picnic lunch,
I have a hunch
It's time we headed out.
O picnic lunch,
Let's grab a bunch
Of food for our new picnic.

Just grab a basket; pack it up.
Then get a blanket. Hurry up!

Round up your friends
And then let's spend
Our picnic lunch together.

—Vicki Dabrowka

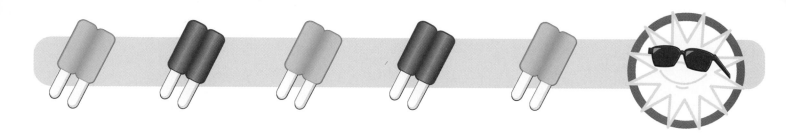

PICNIC FUN

(sung to the tune of "Twinkle, Twinkle, Little Star")

Picnics are a lot of fun
In the nice, warm summer sun.
We can bring good things to eat.
Watermelon—what a treat!
Picnics are a lot of fun.
Come on, now, let's go on one!

—Deborah Garmon

PICNIC PACKING

(sung to the tune of "A-Tisket, A-Tasket")

A picnic! A picnic!
We're going on a picnic!
In the basket I will pack
(Fried chicken) for our picnic!

Repeat the song, substituting different picnic fare each time.

—Ada Goren

WE'RE GOING ON A PICNIC

(sung to the tune of "She'll Be Comin' Round the Mountain")

Oh, we're going on a picnic.
Want to come?
Oh, we're going on a picnic.
Want to come?
Oh, we're going on a picnic,
And it's going to be terrific.
Oh, we're going on a picnic.
Want to come?

—Donna Getzinger

PICNIC DAY

(sung to the tune of "Jingle Bells")

Verse:
Dashing through the store
In a happy sort of mood,
Filling up our cart
With yummy picnic food.
We're going to the park
With coolers packed up tight.
What fun it is to plan a day
Of picnicking outside!

Chorus:
Oh, picnic day, picnic day,
Picnic all the way!
Lay a blanket, toss a ball,
And picnic all the day!
Picnic day, picnic day,
Picnic all the way!
Lay a blanket, toss a ball,
And picnic all the way!

—Michelle McCormick

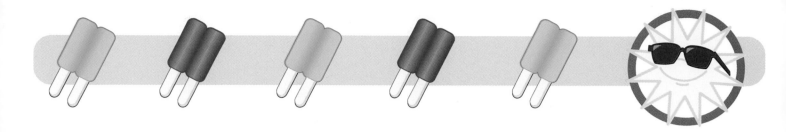

ALL THROUGH THE DAY

(sung to the tune of "The Wheels on the Bus")

The parents at the picnic say, "Come and get it!
Come and get it! Come and get it!"
The parents at the picnic say, "Come and get it!"
All through the day.

The children at the picnic say, "Yum, yum, yum!
Yum, yum, yum! Yum, yum, yum!"
The children at the picnic say, "Yum, yum, yum!"
All through the day.

The dogs at the picnic give happy licks,
Happy licks, happy licks.
The dogs at the picnic give happy licks
All through the day.

The ants at the picnic say, "Thanks for the crumbs!"
Thanks for the crumbs! Thanks for the crumbs!"
The ants at the picnic say, "Thanks for the crumbs!"
All through the day.

—Roxanne LaBell Dearman

JUICY WATERMELON

(sung to the tune of "Clementine")

Watermelon, watermelon,
Watermelon—cool and sweet.
Watermelon is a juicy,
Drippy summer treat to eat.

—Lucia Kemp Henry

SUMMER TREAT
(poem)

Watermelon, summer treat.
Cut a chunk for me to eat.
Tastes so good,
But not too neat!
Watermelon can't be beat!

—Kimberly A. Minafo

WATERMELON SEEDS

(sung to the tune of "Jack and Jill")

Watermelon—juicy, red.
It makes me want to shout!
Cut it open, take a bite,
And then spit the seeds right out!

—Ada Goren

WATCH ME!

(sung to the tune of "Row, Row, Row Your Boat")

Swim, swim, swim all day
In the swimming pool.
Watch me (make a big splash).
Swimming is so cool!

Repeat the song, encouraging children to substitute other swimming-related actions, such as jump in feet first, do the dog paddle, and go underwater.

—Suzanne Moore

WE'RE COOL!

(sung to the tune of "If You're Happy and You Know It")

Oh, we're (swimming) in the pool, in the pool.
Oh, we're (swimming) in the pool, in the pool.
When we're (swimming) in the pool,
The weather's hot but we are cool!
Oh, we're (swimming) in the pool, in the pool.

Repeat the song, encouraging children to substitute other pool-related actions, such as wading, splashing, jumping, and floating.

—Lucia Kemp Henry

THE SWIMMING HOLE

(sung to the tune of "Pawpaw Patch")

Summer's here; time to go swimming.
Summer's here; time to go swimming.
Summer's here; time to go swimming
Way down yonder at the swimming hole!

Stick my toe in. Brr! It's cold.
Stick my toe in. Brr! It's cold.
Stick my toe in. Brr! It's cold
Way down yonder at the swimming hole!

Hold my nose and jump right in.
Hold my nose and jump right in.
Hold my nose and jump right in
Way down yonder at the swimming hole!

Make a big splash; watch it go.
Make a big splash; watch it go.
Make a big splash; watch it go
Way down yonder at the swimming hole!

Encourage your students to make up additional original verses!

—Suzanne Moore

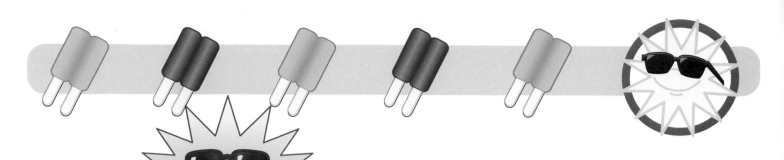

ICE-CREAM FAVORITES

(sung to the tune of "For He's a Jolly Good Fellow")

Oh, (A.J.) likes to eat ice cream.
(A.J.) likes to eat ice cream.
(A.J.) likes to eat ice cream.
And he likes (chocolate chip) the best!

For each verse, choose a child to sing about and have her fill in her favorite ice-cream flavor.

—Ada Goren

ICE CREAM ANY WAY

(sung to the tune of "Daisy, Daisy")

Ice cream, ice cream,
My favorite summer treat!
Cold and frosty,
It sure beats the summer heat!
I love it in a cone
Or in a bowl alone
Or in a shake
Or with birthday cake.
It's my favorite summer treat!

—Ada Goren

LET'S GO ON A VACATION!

(sung to the tune of "Take Me Out to the Ballgame")

Let's go on a vacation.
Let's go somewhere that's fun.
We could travel by car, boat, or train.
We could even fly high in a plane.
So let's just go on a vacation—
Anywhere that is fun.
Pack your bags and we're ready to go
In the summer sun!

—Ada Goren

MY SUMMER VACATION

(sung to the tune of "Hush, Little Baby")

On my vacation, what will I see—
The top of a mountain or the deep blue sea?
On my vacation, how will I go—
Fly in the sky or drive down below?
On my vacation, what will I do—
Swim at the beach or hike through a zoo?
I'm sure that I'll have lots of fun
'Cause this is my summer vacation!

—Donna Getzinger